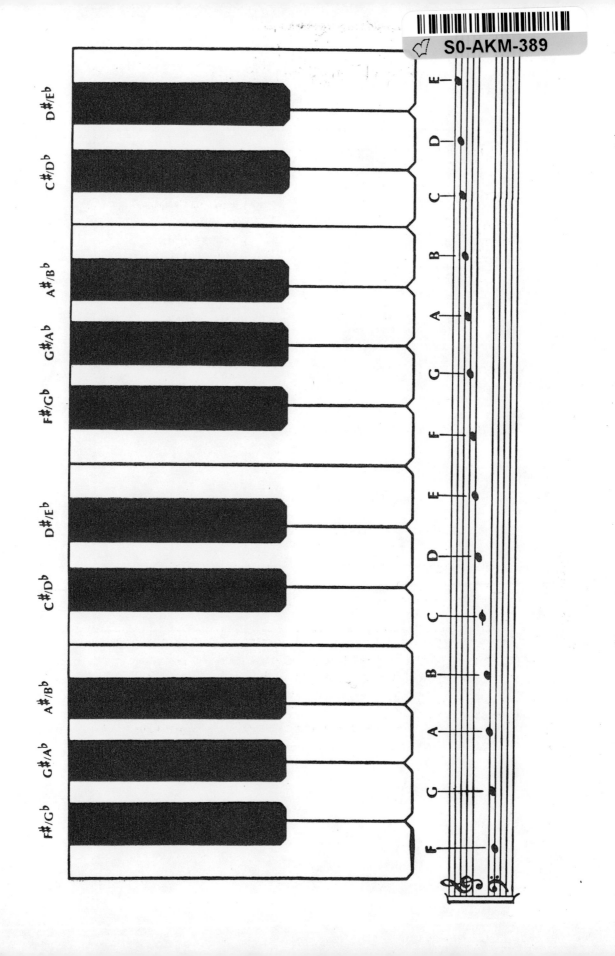

Silver Burdett
music
Centennial Edition

Elizabeth Crook

Bennett Reimer

David S. Walker

SILVER BURDETT COMPANY MORRISTOWN, NEW JERSEY

ATLANTA, GA · CINCINNATI, OH · DALLAS, TX · NORTHFIELD, IL · SAN CARLOS, CA · AGINCOURT, ONTARIO

Contents

MOVE

Clap your hands to the steady beat.

How else can you move to the steady beat?

 "I Clap My Hands"

2

PLAY

As you listen to "I Clap My Hands," play the steady beat on an instrument. You can play steady beats

 on sticks,

 a tambourine,

 or a woodblock.

Here are some patterns you can play. Which pattern will you choose?

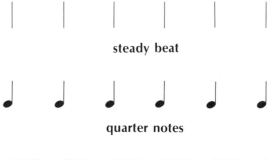

steady beat

quarter notes

eighth notes

eighth notes and quarter notes

3

SING

How will your voice go at the end of the song?

The notes in the color box will tell you.

Marching to Pretoria

DUTCH FOLK SONG FROM SOUTH AFRICA

ENGLISH WORDS BY JOSEF MARAIS
FROM SONGS FROM THE VELD. © 1942, G. SCHIRMER, INC. USED BY PERMISSION.

1. I'm with you and you're with me, And so we are all to-geth-er,
2. We have food, the food is good, And so we will eat to-geth-er,

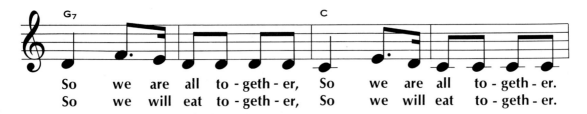

So we are all to-geth-er, So we are all to-geth-er.
So we will eat to-geth-er, So we will eat to-geth-er.

Sing with me, I'll sing with you, And so we will sing to-geth-er,
When we eat, 'twill be a treat, And so let us sing to-geth-er,

As we march a - long.
As we march a - long.

REFRAIN

We are march - ing to Pre - to - ri - a, _____

Pre - to - ri - a, _____ Pre - to - ri - a, _____

4

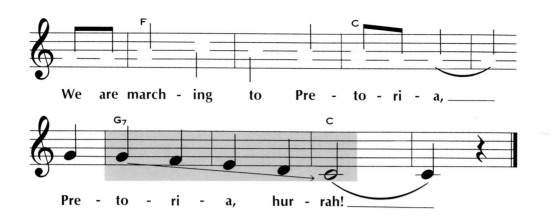

We are march - ing   to   Pre - to - ri - a, _____

Pre - to - ri - a,   hur - rah! _____

Play the ending on the bells. Start on the G bell and
play down to the C bell.

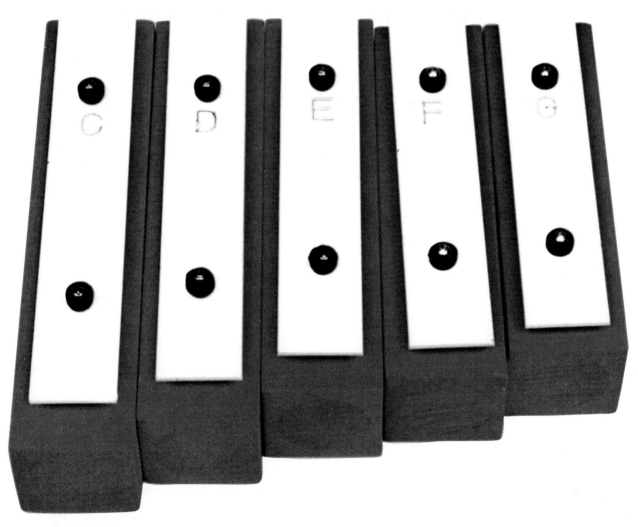

UPWARD, DOWNWARD

Be a music detective. Does the ending of this song move upward, or downward?

Follow the notes as you listen to the recording. When you get to the question mark, move your hand in the air to show how the notes move.

Brother Noah AMERICAN SEA SONG

REPRINTED FROM AMERICAN SEA SONGS AND CHANTEYS, COMPILED BY FRANK SHAY AND ILLUSTRATED BY EDWARD A. WILSON. BY PERMISSION OF W. W. NORTON & COMPANY, INC. COPYRIGHT 1948 BY FRANK SHAY AND EDWARD A. WILSON. COPYRIGHT RENEWED 1976.

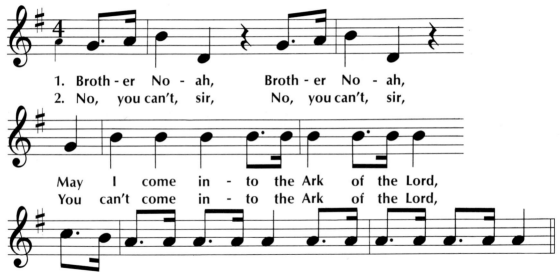

1. Broth - er No - ah,   Broth - er No - ah,
2. No, you can't, sir,   No, you can't, sir,

May   I   come   in - to   the Ark   of   the Lord,
You can't come   in - to   the Ark   of   the Lord,

For   it's grow - ing ver - y dark   and   it's rain - ing ver - y hard?
Though it's grow - ing ver - y dark   and   it's rain - ing ver - y hard.

REFRAIN

Hal - le - loo,   hal - le - loo,   hal - le - loo - oo - oo - oo - ia!

Do you see what you hear? Which pattern of notes shows the part that is missing in the music?

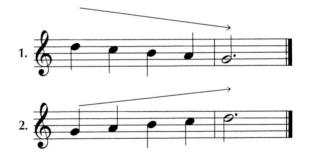

1.
2.

Which part of "Brother Noah" can you play on these bells?

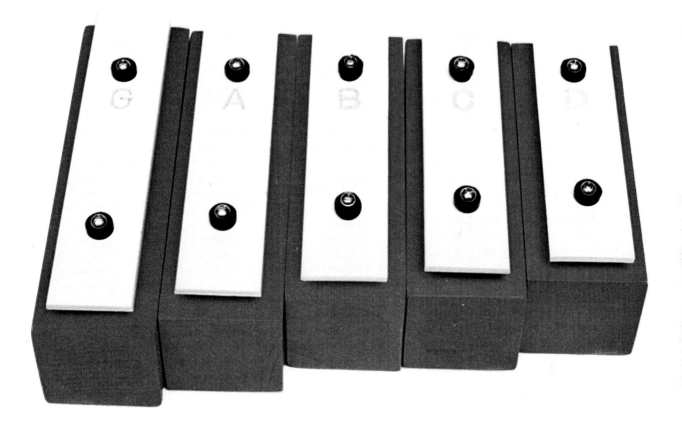

You can play the ending of the song.

Start on the D bell and play down to the G bell.

D   C   B   A   G

EXPERIMENT

Find out which bells play high tones and which bells play low tones.

UPWARD AND DOWNWARD

Listen for the places where the melody goes upward
and downward in this old American fiddle tune.

Old Joe Clark

AMERICAN FOLK SONG   WORDS BY RAYMOND MATTHEWS

1. Old Joe Clark, he built a house, Took him 'bout a week;

He built the floors a-bove his head, The ceil-ings un-der his feet.

REFRAIN

Rock - a - rock, Old Joe Clark, Rock - a - rock, I'm gone;

Rock - a - rock, Old Joe Clark, Good-by, Lu - cy Long.

2. Old Joe Clark, he had a dog
Like none you've ever seen;
With floppy ears and curly tail,
And six feet in between. *Refrain*

3. Old Joe Clark, he had a wife,
Her name was Betty Sue;
She had two great big brown eyes,
The other two were blue. *Refrain*

Pity the Poor Patat

WORDS AND MUSIC BY JOSEF MARAIS. (ASCAP)

MELODY BASED ON AN AFRICAN FOLK TUNE

COPYRIGHT 1946, 1956 FIDEREE MUSIC CO. USED BY PERMISSION.

Can you guess what a *patat* is? The words of the song will give you a clue.

2. The tree, he has his trunk,
   He stares up in the sky.
   Pity the poor patat,
   He can't see with his eye.

3. The tree, he has his leaves,
   They're waving all around.
   Pity the poor patat,
   For he lives in the ground.

4. Although the tree is proud,
   He only gives us wood,
   But from the poor patat
   We get our daily food.

Play the ending of the song on the bells. The notes in the color box will tell you how.

9

The Tree in the Wood

FOLK SONG FROM ENGLAND

Can you find another place where the notes move upward like those in the color box?

1. All in___ a___ wood there grew a tree,
2. And on___ this___ tree there grew a limb,

The fin - est___ tree you ev - er did see;
The fin - est___ limb you ev - er did see;

Repeat for additional lines in verses 3–8.

The tree was in the wood,   The tree was in the wood,
The limb was on the tree,

And the green leaves grew all a-round, a-round, a-round,

And the green leaves grew all a-round.

3. And on this limb there was a branch,

   The finest branch you ever did see;

   The branch was on the limb,

   The limb was on the tree,

   The tree was in the wood,

   And the green leaves grew . . .

4. And on this branch there was a nest, . . .

5. And in this nest there was an egg, . . .

6. And in this egg there was a bird, . . .

7. And on this bird there was a wing, . . .

8. And on this wing there was a feather, . . .

Join into the Game

WORDS AND MUSIC BY PAUL CAMPBELL

Join into the game in your own way.

1. Let ev - 'ry - one clap hands like me. (*clap hands*)
2. Let ev - 'ry - one whis - tle like me. (*whistle*)

Let ev - 'ry - one clap hands like me. (*clap hands*)
Let ev - 'ry - one whis - tle like me. (*whistle*)

REFRAIN

Come on and join in - to the game;_____
Come on and join in - to the game;_____

You'll find that it's al - ways the same. (*clap hands*)
You'll find that it's al - ways the same. (*whistle*)

3. Let ev'ryone laugh like me, (*laugh*)

4. Let ev'ryone sneeze like me, (*sneeze*)

5. Let ev'ryone yawn like me, (*yawn*)

6. Let ev'ryone do what he wants,
   (*various sounds*)

11

TWO DIFFERENT SECTIONS

Roll an' Rock BLACK SPIRITUAL

Ⓐ

Oh, tell me,___ Mar-tha,___ Mar-tha, won't you tell me,

Where have___ you been so long?

Been a-roll-in' an' a-rock-in' at the old church gate,

An' my soul wants to go home to glo - ry.

How will *you* move when the "roll an' rock" part comes in the song?

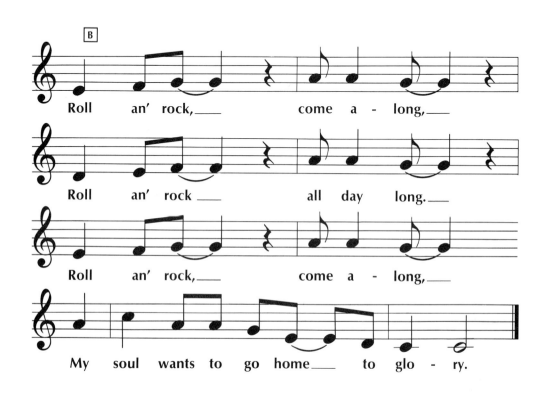

B

Roll an' rock,___ come a - long,___

Roll an' rock ___ all day long.___

Roll an' rock,___ come a - long,___

My soul wants to go home___ to glo - ry.

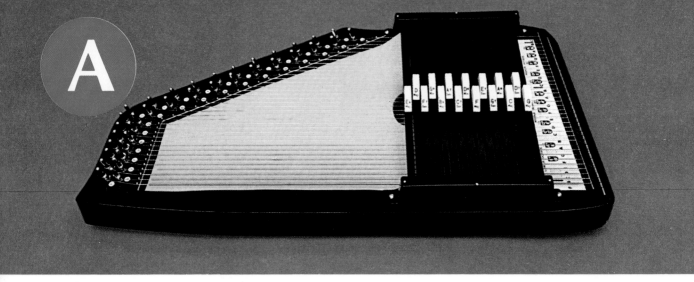

A

Autoharp

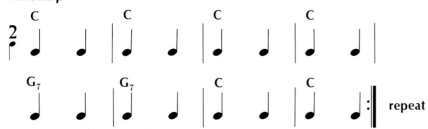

C   C   C   C

G₇   G₇   C   C   : repeat

B

Play instruments to show the A and B sections in "Marching to Pretoria."

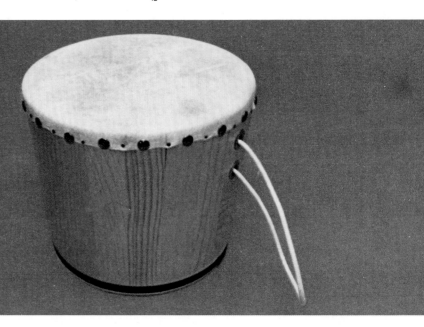

Drum

: repeat

14

Old Dan Tucker

AMERICAN FOLK SONG

Old Dan Tuck - er was a might - y man,

He washed his face in the fry - ing pan,

Combed his hair with a wag - on wheel,

Had a tooth - ache in his heel;

So get out the way, Old Dan Tuck - er;

Get out the way, Old Dan Tuck - er;

Get out the way, Old Dan Tuck - er,

You're too late to get your sup - per.

15

CHANT A PATTERN

Who is your favorite make-believe character?

The title of this song tells you the name of another make-believe character. Chant the name over and over.

Old   Tan - te   Ko - ba

Listen for the "Old Tante Koba" pattern in the recording. Do you hear the pattern in section A or section B?

Old Tante Koba

WORDS AND MUSIC BY JOSEF MARAIS. (ASCAP)

1. Old Tan - te Ko - ba she ought to know,
2. Old Tan - te Ko - ba she loves to eat,

She stirs her cof - fee with her own big toe.
She got so fat____ she can't see her feet.

Old Tan - te Ko - ba she is so dumb,
Old Tan - te Ko - ba she eats a - lone,

She thinks it's bet - ter than to use her thumb.
So no one knows____ that she nibbles the bone.

'Tis - n't my af - fair,____ 'tis - n't your af - fair,____

It's Tan - te Ko - ba's trou - bles so we need - n't care.

'Tis - n't my af - fair,____ 'tis - n't your af - fair,____

It's Tan - te Ko - ba's trou - bles so we need - n't care.

Here are two rhythm patterns to play with the song.
You can play the "Old Tante Koba" pattern in section
A or the steady beat pattern in section B. Which will
you choose?

TONE COLOR

Instrumental Parts for "Mama Paquita" ⊚ 1

claves

drum

guitar

cowbell

maracas

Your voice has its own special sound. Add the tone color of *your* voice as you sing with the recording.

Mama Paquita

CARNIVAL SONG FROM BRAZIL   ENGLISH WORDS BY MARGARET MARKS ⊚ 1

1. Ma - ma Pa - qui - ta, Ma - ma Pa - qui - ta,

Ma - ma Pa - qui - ta, buy your ba - by a pa - pa - ya,

A ripe pa - pa - ya   and a ba - na - na,

A ripe ba - na - na that your ba - by will en - joy, ma - ma - ma - ma,

Ma - ma Pa - qui - ta,   Ma - ma Pa - qui - ta,

Ma - ma Pa - qui - ta says, "I have - n't an - y mon - ey

To buy pa - pa - yas   and ripe ba - na - nas,

Let's go   to Car - ni - val and dance the night a - way!"

2. Mama Paquita, Mama Paquita,

Mama Paquita, buy your baby some pajamas,

Some new pajamas, and a sombrero,

A new sombrero that your baby will enjoy, ma-ma-ma-ma,

Mama Paquita, Mama Paquita,

Mama Paquita says, "I haven't any money

To buy pajamas and a sombrero,

Let's go to Carnival and dance the night away!"

Look at the notes in the color boxes. Use your arms to show how the notes move.

Michie Banjo

CREOLE BAMBOULA   ENGLISH WORDS BY MARGARET MARKS

Look at Mich-ie Ban-jo, Fan-cy Mich-ie Ban-jo,

Strut-tin'___ down the street.   1. *Cha-peau*___ cocked on one
                                  2. Dia-mond___ pin in his

side, Mich-ie Ban-jo, High but-ton shoes that squeak,
tie, Mich-ie Ban-jo, Bright yel-low gloves so neat,

Walk-in' stick a-swing-in' wide, Mich-ie Ban-jo,
Trou-sers pleat-ed way up high, Mich-ie Ban-jo,

Ev-'ry-thing's all com-plete.
Ev-'ry-thing's all com-plete.

But the Cat Came Back

WORDS AND MUSIC BY JOSEF MARAIS, (ASCAP)

(A) VERSE

1. Fred-die Wil-son had a cat that he did-n't want to keep.

He of-fered him for free and he tried to sell him cheap.

He called up-on the preach-er one Sun-day for ad-vice;

The preach-er said, "Yes, leave him here, it would be so nice!"

B REFRAIN

But the cat came back, he would-n't stay a-way,

He was sit-ting on the porch on the ver-y next day.

The cat came back, he did-n't want to roam,

The ver-y next day it was "Home, Sweet Home."

2. Freddie put him on a ship and they headed for Ceylon.
   The ship was overloaded more than twenty thousand ton.
   Not far away from shore the cargo ship went down,
   There wasn't any doubt about it, everybody drowned. *Refrain*

3. Then he put the cat aboard with a man in a balloon,
   Who would give the cat away to the man in the moon.
   The balloon it didn't rise, it burst in bits instead,
   And ten miles from the spot, they found the man stone dead. *Refrain*

THE AUTOHARP

Lady, Come   FOLK SONG FROM ENGLAND

La - dy, come, Can't you see?

John fell off the white oak tree.

Play a harmony part on the Autoharp.

Press the G button with the pointer finger of your left hand.

Strum the strings with your right hand.

Try this strumming pattern.

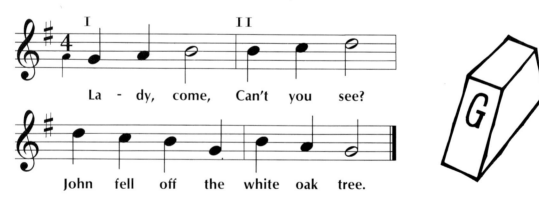

It uses long sounds.

MUSIC FOR AUTOHARP

Listen to a sound piece for Autoharp.   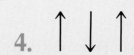 *Autoharp Sound Piece*

Then, make up a sound piece of your own.

SOUND PIECE 1: *Autoharp Design*   DAVID S. WALKER

TRY
- Plucking strings
- Strumming strings
- Playing with hard mallet
- Playing with soft mallet
- Playing with plastic pick
- Playing with felt pick
- Sliding a comb along strings
- Sliding a ruler along strings
- Tapping wood case
- Rubbing strings with fingertips

PLAY
- High sounds
- Low sounds
- Sounds from high to low
- Sounds from low to high
- Several high sounds together
- Several low sounds together
- Loud sounds
- Soft sounds
- Long sounds
- Short sounds

Can you play this notation on the Autoharp?

1.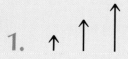

2. • • • •

3. • • • •

4. ↑ ↓ ↑

A TOE-TAPPING SONG

This fiddle tune will keep your feet a-hoppin'.

Tap your toe to the steady beat as you listen to the recording.

Ain't Gonna Rain   AMERICAN FOLK SONG

1. The wood-chuck, he's a - chop-pin' wood,

The pos - sum, he's a - haul - in'.

My poor old dog fell off a log And killed him - self a - bawl - in'.

REFRAIN

It ain't gon-na rain, it ain't gon-na rain, It ain't gon-na rain no more.

Come on down, ev - 'ry-bod-y sing. It ain't gon-na rain no more.

2. Just bake them biscuits good and brown,
   It ain't gonna rain no more.
   Swing your ladies round and round,
   It ain't gonna rain no more. *Refrain*

3. I'll tune the fiddle, you get the bow,
   It ain't gonna rain no more.
   The weatherman just told me so,
   It ain't gonna rain no more. *Refrain*

4. Oh, what did the blackbird say to the crow?
   "It ain't gonna rain no more.
   It ain't gonna hail, it ain't gonna snow,
   It ain't gonna rain no more." *Refrain*

24

ADD A HARMONY PART

Can you play a harmony part for "Ain't Gonna Rain"?
Find the G and D_7 buttons on the Autoharp. The
letters over the notes will tell you when to play
each chord.

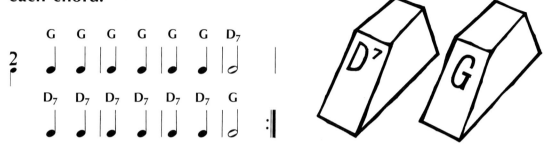

Sweetly Sings the Donkey ROUND

What would you expect the donkey to say? Be ready
to sing the Hee-haw parts in this song.

Sweet - ly sings the don - key   at   the break of day;

If   you   do   not feed   him,   this   is what he'll say,

"Hee-haw!   Hee-haw!   Hee - haw! Hee - haw! Hee - haw!"

Follow the letter names in the music and play a
harmony part. Which chord buttons will you need to
press?

LOOK

Long ago, shepherds
played pipes that
looked like these.

LISTEN

Another kind of pipe
is called a *recorder*.

In the picture, you see
a group of recorders.

Listen to them

play together.

⊙ Anonymous:

Dadme Albricias, Hijos d'Eva

26

PLAY

You can play a pipe called a *soprano recorder.*

Hold the recorder with both hands, with the left hand on top.

COVER-THE-HOLE TEST
Press just hard enough so the hole will make a light mark on each finger of your left hand.

MAKING A SOUND
Cover the tip of the mouthpiece with your lips.
Blow gently through the recorder, starting to blow with a "daah."

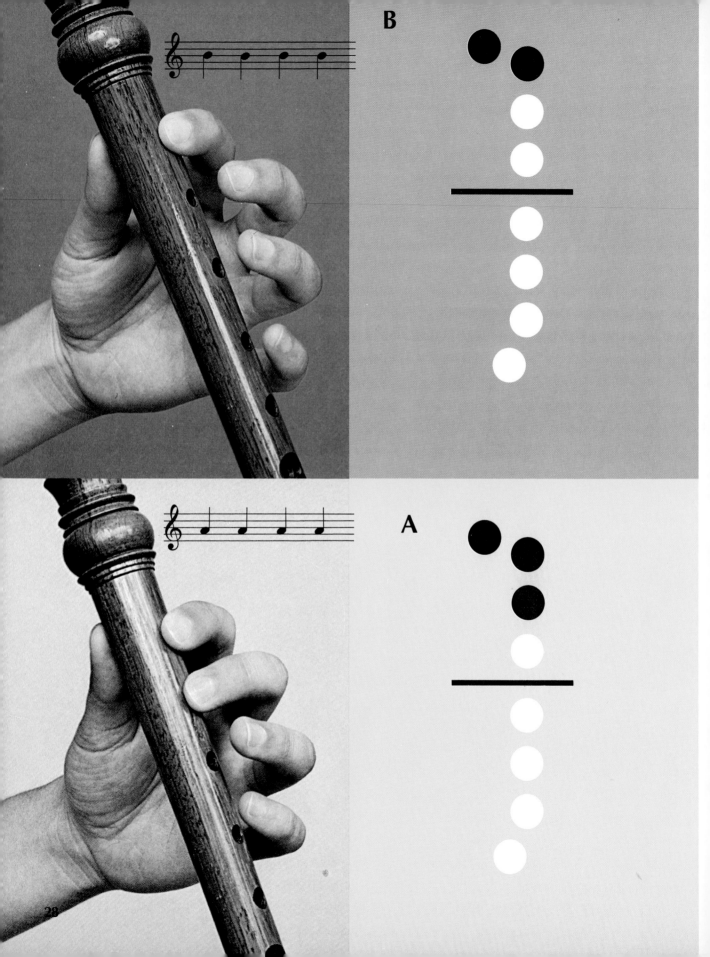

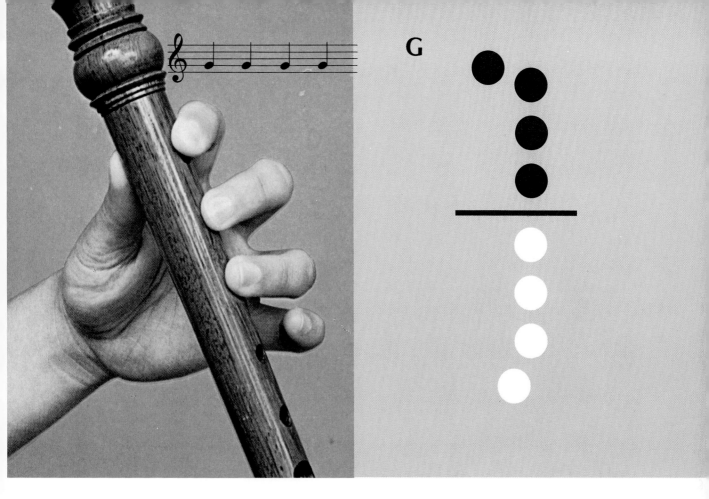

G

Look at the pictures on pages 28 and 29 to see which fingers you will use to play the tones B, A, and G.

Cover the holes with your fingers. Now blow gently four times for each tone. Start each blow with a "daah."

When you are ready, play a recorder part with the melody of "Ain't Gonna Rain." You will be playing a countermelody.

Recorder

Can you find a sign that tells you where the line G is on the staff?

THINGS TO DO WITH B A G
ON A RECORDER

1. Fill in the silences in "Mama Paquita," playing

G   G   G   G   A   G

2. Play this pattern throughout "Lady, Come."

3. Play G throughout the first section of "Marching to Pretoria," using

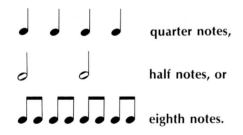

quarter notes,

half notes, or

eighth notes.

4. Play a countermelody with "Brother Noah."

MORE THINGS TO DO WITH B A G

Here are two songs you can play on your recorder. One is a bouncy little melody. The other is a quiet, gentle song. Practice both of them. Each one starts on B.

Lullaby FRENCH FOLK MELODY

Go to sleep, you dear lit - tle ba - by.

Close your eyes and go _____ to sleep.

Hop, Old Squirrel BLACK-AMERICAN SINGING GAME

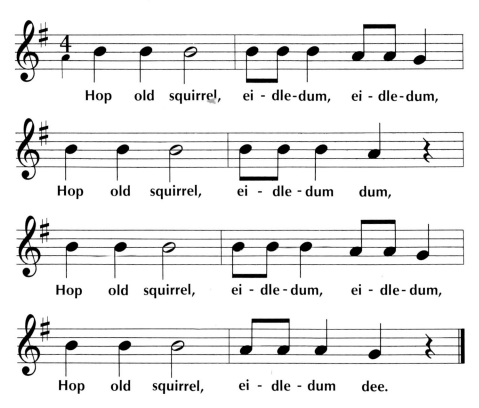

Hop old squirrel, ei - dle-dum, ei - dle-dum,

Hop old squirrel, ei - dle - dum dum,

Hop old squirrel, ei - dle-dum, ei - dle-dum,

Hop old squirrel, ei - dle-dum dee.

MELODY AND HARMONY

1. A melody sung alone has no harmony.

2. A melody with chords has harmony.

3. A melody sung as a round has harmony.

Sing Together

OLD ENGLISH ROUND

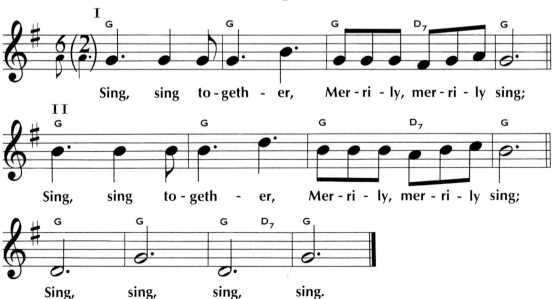

USE YOUR EARS

"A Ram Sam Sam" is performed three ways on the recording. As you listen, point to the diagram on page 32 that shows what you are hearing.

A Ram Sam Sam FOLK SONG FROM MOROCCO

A ram sam sam, a ram sam sam,
Gu - li gu - li gu - li gu - li gu - li ram sam sam.
A ra - fi, a ra - fi,
Gu - li gu - li gu - li gu - li gu - li ram sam sam.

Sing "A Ram Sam Sam" with no harmony. Add Autoharp chords for harmony.

Listen to two pieces for instruments. Which piece has harmony? Which has no harmony?

Smith: *Three Brevities for Solo Flute*

Sor: *Variations on a Theme by Mozart*

33

FOLLOW-THE-LEADER GAME

Che Che Koolay

SINGING GAME FROM GHANA

FROM HI, NEIGHBOR (BOOK 2) BY UNITED STATES
FOR UNICEF, UNITED NATIONS, N.Y.
USED BY PERMISSION.

2

Follow the phrases as you sing.

Are they the same length, or different?

As you play the game, feel the length of each phrase.

LEADER

Che-che koo-lay

(Hands on head)

Che-che ko-fee sa

(Hands on shoulders)

Ko-fee sa-lan-ga

(Hands on hips)

Ka-ka-shee lan-ga

(Hands on knees)

Koom-ma-dye-day

(Grasp ankles)

Che-che koo-lay

Che-che ko-fee sa

Ko-fee sa-lan-ga

Ka-ka-shee lan-ga

Koom-ma-dye-day

35

The Arts:
Movement

Mathieu: *Painting*

What part of this painting seems to be lively and active?

What part seems to have little or no movement?

Listen to these two pieces of music. In one, the music is mostly still. In the other, it is active.

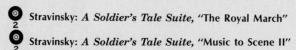

Stravinsky: *A Soldier's Tale Suite,* "The Royal March"

Stravinsky: *A Soldier's Tale Suite,* "Music to Scene II"

The Solomon R. Guggenheim Museum Collection: Georges Mathieu: PAINTING, 1952.

You *see* things in a painting all at once.

You *hear* things in music over a span of time.

37

LISTENING TO MUSIC

How do you hear sounds? Be very still and listen to the sounds around you.

As you listen to "Kites Are Fun," think about what you hear.

Dedrick, Chris: *Kites Are Fun*

> A group sings the song. There are both men's and
> women's voices in the group.
> The voices are accompanied by instruments.
> The music has a steady beat. It has both long and
> short sounds.

REMEMBER

The more sounds your ears *hear*—

The more sounds you *think* about—

The more sounds you *feel*.

What are these children hearing?

Tempo

Listen to two recordings of this song.

Which is *fast?* Which is *slow?*

Oh, What a Beautiful City

BLACK SPIRITUAL

Oh,   what   a beau - ti - ful   cit - y,____

Oh,   what   a beau - ti - ful   cit - y,____

Sing the song both ways.

Which *tempo* feels right to you?

Which conductor chooses a *faster tempo* for this piece?

Handel: *Water Music,* "Air"
2

Oh,   what   a beau - ti - ful   cit - y, ____

Twelve gates - a to the cit - y, ____ Hal - le - lu - jah!

FASTER-SLOWER-SAME

Something happens to the tempo in the recording of
this song.

Can you think what it might be?

The words will give you a clue.

Listen to the recording to find out if you guessed right.

Hey Ho, Hey Lo

SLOVAKIAN FOLK TUNE   ENGLISH WORDS BY RAYMOND MATTHEWS

Hey ho, hey lo, tam-bou-rines are ring - ing;

Hey ho, hey lo, ring - ing all a - round.

Lis - ten, lis - ten, hear them jin - gle jan - gle,

Mak - ing mu - sic with a hap - py sound.

Fast - er, fast - er, how they jin - gle jan - gle,

Mak - ing mu - sic with a hap - py sound.

As you listen to "Speed of the Beat," think of how you will move to the music. Reimer: *Speed of the Beat*

Wind Up the Apple Tree

AMERICAN SINGING GAME

FROM SINGING GAMES AND PLAYPARTY GAMES BY RICHARD CHASE, DOVER PUBLICATIONS, INC., NEW YORK, 1949, 1967. REPRINTED THROUGH THE PERMISSION OF THE PUBLISHER.

Does the beat get faster, or slower, in this song?

Wind up the ap - ple tree! Hold on tight!

Wind it all___ day___ and wind it all___ night!

Faster

Stir up the dump - lings, the pot boils o - ver!

Can you hear the beat change in this music?

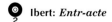 Ibert: *Entr-acte*

STOP AND HOLD

Can you hear the beat stop and hold in this song?
Can you find the sign that tells you when to stop
and hold?

Carrot Stew

WORDS AND MUSIC BY LARRY GROCE

1. When-ev-er we have a friend for lunch,

There's just one thing to do.

We pick some ber-ries and catch some fish,

And we make a car-rot stew.

B REFRAIN

Car-rot stew, car-rot stew,

It's our fav'-rite thing to do.

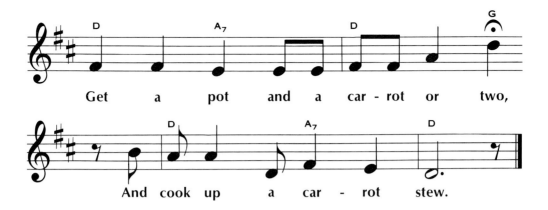

Get a pot and a car-rot or two,

And cook up a car-rot stew.

2. Nothing makes our tummies so full

And keeps us happy too,

As a great big pot or a little bitty bowl

Or a spoonful of carrot stew. *Refrain*

3. So when you come to our little house,

Bring a carrot if you have a few.

We'll put it in a pot 'til it's nice and hot,

And make some carrot stew. *Refrain*

PLAYGROUND CHANTS

Choose one of these rhymes to chant for your friends.
Try different things. Will you chant some lines faster?
Slower? You might even decide to stop and hold on
one or two words.

Hana, mana, mona, mike,

Barcelona, bona, strike,

Hare, ware, frown, venac,

Harrico, warrico, we, wo, wac.

Down by the ocean,

Down by the sea,

Johnnie broke a milk bottle

And blamed it on me.

I told Ma and Ma told Pa.

Johnnie got a licking

With a Ha! Ha! Ha!

How many licks did he get?

1, 2, 3, etc.

Alouette

FOLK SONG FROM CANADA

Clap your hands softly on every beat as you listen to the recording of "Alouette." Notice that the singer stops and holds every time he sings "Oh!"

Find the sign that tells the singer when to stop and hold.

1. Je te plu - me - rai la tête, Je te plu - me - rai la tête,
2. Je te plu - me - rai la bec, Je te plu - me - rai la bec,

(No repeat first time)

1. Et la tête, et la tête.
2. Et la bec, et la bec. A - lou-ette, A - lou-ette. Oh!
   Et la tête, et la tête.

3. Le nez   4. Le dos   5. Les pattes   6. Le cou

When you sing "Alouette," tap the steady beat on a tambourine. How will you play the tambourine on the stop-and-hold note?

46

WHAT DO YOU HEAR? 1: *Tempo* ⊚₂

**Listen to this music. Circle the word that best describes
what is happening to the beat.
Is it fast, or slow? Is it getting faster, or getting slower?**

1.	*FAST*	*SLOW*
2.	*GETTING FASTER*	*GETTING SLOWER*
3.	*FAST*	*SLOW*
4.	*FAST*	*SLOW*
5.	*GETTING FASTER*	*GETTING SLOWER*

Train Ride

**Now listen to the music on this recording.
Circle the word that best describes the tempo.
Is it fast, or slow? Do you hear the beat stop and hold?
If you do, circle ⌢. If you do not, circle NO ⌢.**

1.	*FAST*	*SLOW*	⌢	*NO* ⌢
2.	*FAST*	*SLOW*	⌢	*NO* ⌢
3.	*FAST*	*SLOW*	⌢	*NO* ⌢
4.	*FAST*	*SLOW*	⌢	*NO* ⌢

Beethoven: *Violin Concerto,* "Rondo"
Alouette

Chopin: *Sonata in B♭ Minor,* "Funeral March"
Haydn: *Quartet in D Minor,* Movement 4

47

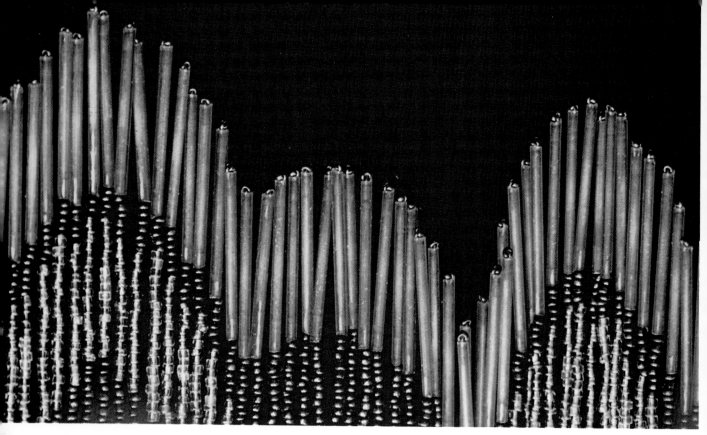

Melody

With the tip of one finger, trace the outline made by
the top of the design. Notice that your finger goes
upward and downward.

Now trace the outline made by the arrows on each staff.
Notice when they go upward and when they go downward.

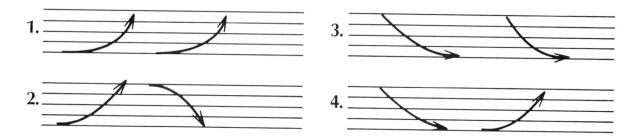

Choose one of the staffs. Play a swooping sound on the bells
or on the keyboard in the same direction as the arrows.

Follow the lines as you hear the sound moving upward and downward on the recording.

🔘
2 *Electronic Sounds 1 and 2*

Do you see what you hear? Which line shows what you hear next?

🔘
2 *Hearing Electronic Sounds*

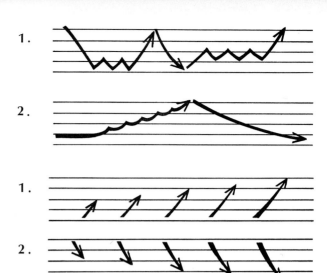

Look at the notes in the color boxes. Does the ending of each phrase move in an upward direction, or a downward direction?

All the Pretty Little Horses FOLK SONG FROM SOUTHERN UNITED STATES 🔘 3

Hush - a - by, don't you cry, Go to sleep-y, lit -tle ba - by.

When you wake, you shall have All the pret-ty lit - tle hors - es:

Blacks and bays, dap-ples and grays, Coach and six - a lit-tle hors - es.

Hush - a - by, don't you cry, Go to sleep-y, lit-tle ba - by.

A MELODY PATTERN FOR BELLS

Play this pattern on the bells.

You will need the B, A, and G bells.

Do the notes move in a downward,

or an upward direction?

B   A   G

Find the pattern in the color box in the first line of "Clover." Can you find the same pattern in two other places in the song?

Clover

FOLK SONG FROM CZECHOSLOVAKIA   ENGLISH WORDS BY RAYMOND MATTHEWS

1. Clo - ver's grow - ing here;   Clo - ver's grow - ing there.

Now the win - ter's o - ver, Fields are green with clo - ver

Grow - ing ev - 'ry - where.   Now the win - ter's o - ver,

Fields are green with clo - ver Grow - ing ev - ry - where.

2. Clover smells so sweet. (*2 times*)

When the day is fair,

Its fragrance fills the air,   } (*2 times*)

The clover smells so sweet.

3. Clover has three leaves. (*2 times*)

If a fourth one's there,

You'll find it's very rare,   } (*2 times*)

For clover has three leaves.

FOLLOW THE SCORE

Can you guess what instrument plays the melody on the recording of this piece? The title may give you a clue.

Follow the upward and downward direction of the notes with your finger as you listen to the recording.

Pipe in D Major
ALBERT ROUSSEL

A MELODY PATTERN TO SING

How will you use your voice when you sing this

spooky song? The words may give you an idea.

Skin and Bones

FOLK SONG FROM KENTUCKY   COLLECTED BY JEAN RITCHIE

© 1952 JEAN RITCHIE. GEORDIE MUSIC PUBLISHING, INC.

1. There was an old wom-an all   skin and bones, Oo - oo - oo-ooh!
2. One night__ she thought__she'd take a walk, Oo - oo - oo-ooh!

She lived down by   the old grave-yard, Oo - oo - oo-ooh! (*To verse 2*)
She walked down by   the old grave-yard, Oo - oo - oo-ooh! (*To verse 3*)

She   o-pened the door   and BOO!!

3. She saw the bones a-layin' around,

Oo-oo-oo-ooh!

She went to the closet to get a broom,

Oo-oo-oo-ooh!   (*To coda*)

Can you find this pattern in "Skin and Bones"?

Play it on the bells every time it comes in the song.

B   A   G   E

To play the pattern on the recorder, you need a new

note, E. Look on page 53 to discover how to play it.

52

NEW NOTE—E

Recorder or Bells

E   B A G

53

FOLLOW THE DIRECTION

Look at the notes in the color box. Can you find
another place in the song where the notes move in
the same way?

Chicka Hanka AMERICAN FOLK SONG

FROM ECHOES OF AFRICA IN FOLK SONGS OF THE AMERICAS. BY BEATRICE LANDECK. COPYRIGHT © 1961, BY BEATRICE LANDECK. PUBLISHED BY DAVID MCKAY COMPANY, INC. REPRINTED BY PERMISSION.

Cap - tain, go side - track your train!____

Cap - tain, go side - track your train!____

Num - ber Three in line, Com - in' in on time,

Cap - tain, go side - track your train!____

Follow the direction of the melody in "Chicka Hanka"
and try playing the whole song on bells or recorder. It
starts on E. Here are the notes you will use.

E   G   A   B

DIRECTION CHECKUP

Here are parts of songs
to play on bells.
Follow the direction of
the melody as you play.

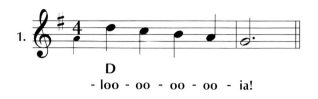

1.
D
- loo - oo - oo - oo - ia!

2.
G
La - dy, come, Can't you see?

3.
D
It ain't gon-na rain no more.

4.
D
Go to sleep-y lit-tle ba - by.

5.
D
He's on - ly got a skin.

6.
B
Oo - oo - oo - ooh!

7.
D
Car - ni - val and dance the night a - way!

8.
C
All in____ a____ wood there grew a tree,

On the First Thanksgiving Day

WORDS TRADITIONAL

MUSIC BY JAKOB HINTZE

What instrument accompanies the children's voices on the recording?

On the first Thanks - giv - ing Day,
Thanked the Lord for sun and rain,

Pil - grims went to church to pray,
Thanked him for the fields of grain.

Now Thanks - giv - ing comes a - gain:

Praise the Lord as they did then.

Thank him for the sun and rain,

Thank him for the fields of grain.

Look at the notes in the color box. Find another place where the notes move downward in the same way.

WHAT DO YOU HEAR? 2: *Melody* ⊚₃

Listen to these pieces of music.

As each number is called, circle the word that best describes the direction the melody is moving. Is it moving *upward,* or *downward,* or both *upward* and *downward?*

---

1. *UPWARD*   *DOWNWARD*
UPWARD AND DOWNWARD

---

2. *UPWARD*   *DOWNWARD*
UPWARD AND DOWNWARD

---

3. *UPWARD*   *DOWNWARD*
UPWARD AND DOWNWARD

Beethoven: *Concerto No. 5 in E♭ Major,* "Emperor," Movement 1

---

1. *UPWARD*   *DOWNWARD*

---

2. *UPWARD*   *DOWNWARD*

---

3. *UPWARD*   *DOWNWARD*

---

4. *UPWARD*   *DOWNWARD*

Gershwin: *Rhapsody in Blue*   Rimsky-Korsakov: *Le Coq D'or*
Ponchielli: *Dance of the Hours*   Kuhlau: *Sonatina*

Composers

Here are four composers.

On the recording, you will hear one of them tell you

what a composer does.

3 Things People Do with Music

Rain Song

WORDS AND MUSIC BY DAVID McHUGH © 1972 DAVID McHUGH

The rain just keeps on fall-ing, And the sky is col-ored grey;

The birds don't stop their sing-ing___ 'Cause it's just an-oth-er day;

And the clouds keep pass-ing o-ver, Bring-in' rain to flow'rs be-low;

While the sun keeps wait-ing pa-tient-ly To un-veil its gold-en glow;

Some-times sun shines, and oth-er times it rains;___

But to me it's all the same,___

To me it's all the same.___

59

Meter

METER IN 2—SETS OF TWO

When you bounce and catch a ball, you make motions in sets of two. In music, these sets are called METER.

  BOUNCE, catch; BOUNCE, catch.

Listen to the recording. Pretend to bounce and catch a ball in time to the steady beat.

New Year's Song *Kazoe-uta* FOLK SONG FROM JAPAN   ENGLISH VERSION BY ROSEMARY JACQUES

1. On the eve of New Year's,___ Bus-y peo-ple, hap-py peo-ple,
Hi - to - tsu to ya,_____ Hi - to - yo a - ku - re - ba,

Run-ning here and there, Run-ning here and there,
Ni - gi - ya - ka de, Ni - gi - ya - ka de,

Dec-o-rate the bam-boo trees to cel-e-brate the day,_____
O - ka - za - ri ta - te - ta - ru ma - tsu - ka - za - ri,_____

Cel-e-brate the day.
Ma - tsu - ka - za - ri.

2. On the eve of New Year's,

   Paper streamers, fresh plum blossoms

   Hang above the door,

   Hang above the door,

   Telling all who pass by

      to have a happy day,

   Have a happy day.

3. On the day of New Year's,

   Games are played and songs are sung

   To celebrate the day,

   Celebrate the day.

   People come to wish each other

      Happy New Year's Day,

   Happy New Year's Day.

ADD A PART
Play one of these parts for instruments while others sing "New Year's Song."

Recorder or Bells

1. E   B   Play throughout

2. E   B   Play throughout

3. E   B   Play throughout

Woodblock   Play throughout

Gong   Play throughout

METER IN 3—SETS OF THREE

Feel the beats in sets of three as you listen to this song.

Find the Ring

FOLK SONG FROM GREECE   ENGLISH WORDS BY MARIA JORDAN

1. Find the ring, the ring that keeps mov - ing,
2. Find the ring, the ring that keeps mov - ing,

Find the ring, oh, where did it go?
Find the ring of sil - ver or gold.

The se - cret ring's in some - bod - y's hand, Some -
Pass it to me, I'll pass it to you, We

bod - y you know, come guess if you can!
must - n't get caught, what - ev - er we do!

Don't say a word if you are the one, Don't

give it a - way and spoil all the fun!

Tambourine

Finger Cymbals

METER IN 3

What sign tells you that this song moves in a
meter of 3?

Sandy McNab

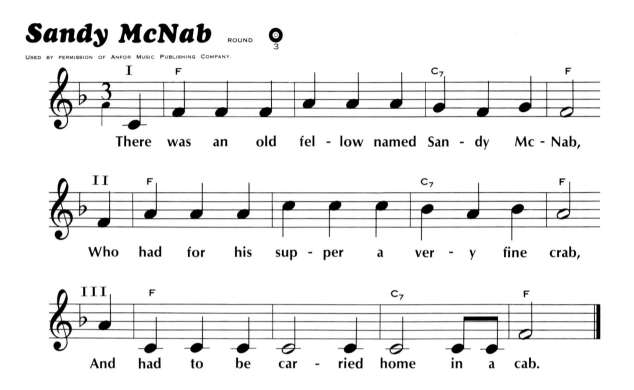

There was an old fel - low named San - dy Mc - Nab,

Who had for his sup - per a ver - y fine crab,

And had to be car - ried home in a cab.

Play the STEADY beat on a woodblock.

Woodblock

Play the STRONG beat on a drum.

Drum

CALL CHART 1: *Meter* 🎵
3

You have sung, played, and heard music in different meters.

Listen to the recording.

As each number is called, look at the chart. It will help

you hear the meter in sets of two and sets of three.

Kingsley: *Piece in Two Meters*

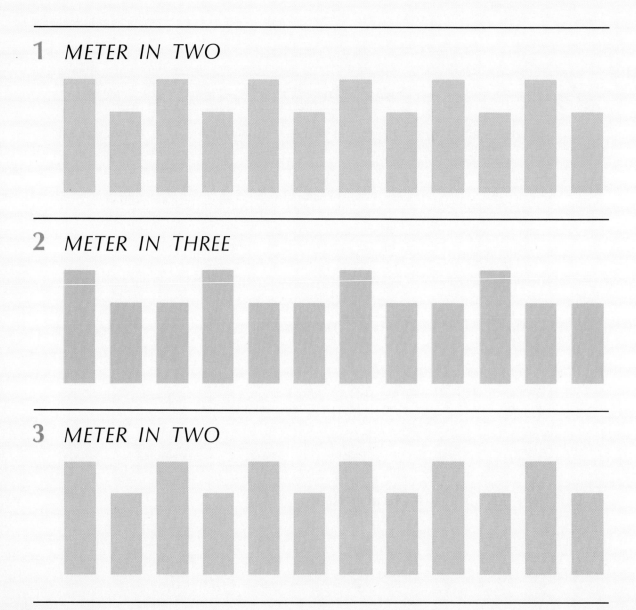

1 *METER IN TWO*

2 *METER IN THREE*

3 *METER IN TWO*

STRONG BEATS

Play a tambourine in section B as you listen to this song.

Hit shake shake Hit shake shake

Which of the three beats is the strongest?

Buying Fish

YIDDISH FOLK SONG   ENGLISH WORDS BY ELIZABETH S. BACHMAN

1. One day his moth-er sent him to mar-ket
2. Moth-er had said, "Go straight to the mar-ket;

To buy some fish____ to fry. ____
Don't lin-ger on ____ the way." ____

But when he got there he could-n't re-mem-ber
But he stopped to watch a game in the park, And

What kind she want-ed him to buy.____
now— oh, dear! what will Moth-er say?____

Day, day, day, day, day, day, Day, day, day, day, day, day,

Day, day, day, day, day, day, Day, day, day, day.

'Taters

YIDDISH FOLK SONG   ENGLISH WORDS BY JACOB SLOAN

Listen for the meter in this song. Do you feel sets of two, or sets of three?

1. Sun - day, 'ta - ters, Mon - day, 'ta - ters,

Tues - day and Wednes - day,___ 'ta - ters,

Thurs - day and Fri - day,___ 'ta - ters,

Sab - bath, for a spe - cial treat, there's a 'ta - ter pud - ding!

Sun - day___ starts with___ 'ta - ters.

2. Bread and 'taters, Meat and 'taters, Lunch and dinner, 'taters.

    Over and over, 'taters.

    Once, for a special treat, there's a 'tater pudding!

    Sunday starts with 'taters.

3. Still, 'taters, Ever, 'taters, Always, always, 'taters!

    Today and tomorrow, 'taters!

    After Sabbath pot roasts there's a 'tater pudding!

    Sunday starts with 'taters.

METER IN 2 OR METER IN 3?

Ging Gong Gooli
FOLK SONG FROM BRITISH GUIANA

Ging gong goo - li goo - li goo - li goo - li wat - cha,

Ging gong goo, ging gong goo.

Ging gong goo - li goo - li goo - li goo - li wat - cha,

Ging gong goo, ging gong goo.

Hai - la, _____ hai - la shai - la, _____

Shai - la hai - la shai - la ho - la - ho!

Hai - la, _____ hai - la shai - la, _____

Shai - la hai - la shai - la ho! _____

Love

WORDS AND MUSIC BY CARMINO RAVOSA   © 1971 CARMINO RAVOSA

3

Pretend to push a swing as you listen to this song. Make
one strong "push" in each measure.

Push___ Push___ Push___ Push___

1. Love   can charm the birds___   right out   of   the   trees,

Love   can take the hon - ey   a - way   from   the   bees;

Love   can make a   li - on stand   up   and   say, "Please."___

2. Love can turn a hurricane into a breeze,

   Love can get a hermit to smile and say, "Cheese";

   Love can make a dog learn to live with his fleas.

3. Love can bring a giant right down to his knees,

   Love can make the North and the South Poles unfreeze;

   Love can make a kid learn to eat all his peas.

Recorder or Bells

G   A

WHAT DO YOU HEAR? 3: *Meter*

Each time a number is called, decide whether the beats are grouped in sets of two, or in sets of three.

If you think the beats are grouped in sets of two, draw a circle around METER IN 2.

If you think the beats are grouped in sets of three, draw a circle around METER IN 3.

Listen. Then circle what you hear.

1	METER IN 2	METER IN 3
2	METER IN 2	METER IN 3
3	METER IN 2	METER IN 3

Kingsley: *Piece in Two Meters*

1	METER IN 2	METER IN 3
2	METER IN 2	METER IN 3
3	METER IN 2	METER IN 3

Ton moulin

Dynamics

Read this poem. Where will you use soft sounds and loud sounds to show that rain comes in different sizes?

RAIN SIZES

Rain comes in various sizes.
Some rain is as small as a mist.
It tickles your face with surprises,
And tingles as if you'd been kissed.

Some rain is the size of a sprinkle
And doesn't put out all the sun.
You can see the drops sparkle and twinkle,
And a rainbow comes out when it's done.

Some rain is as big as a nickle
And comes with a crash and a hiss.
It comes down too heavy to tickle.
It's more like a splash than a kiss.

When it rains the right size and you're
  wrapped in
Your rainclothes, it's fun out of doors.
But run home before you get trapped in
The big rain that rattles and roars.

John Ciardi

Now listen to the recording. How does the reader use *her* voice to make the poem interesting?

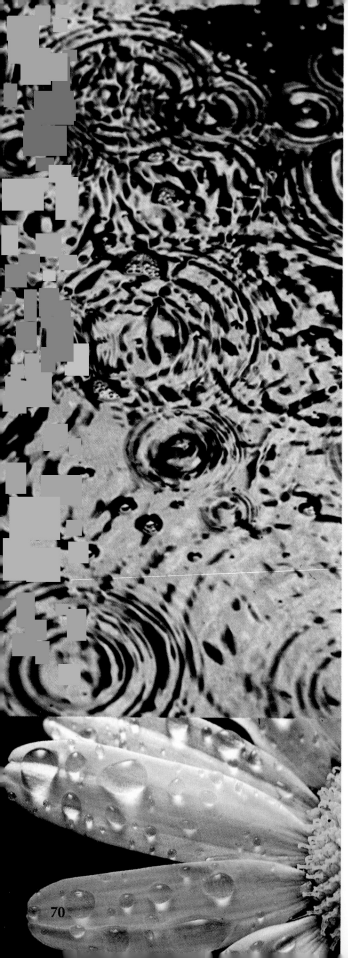

70

Say the words of this song out loud. How will you use your *speaking* voice to describe John's ghost?

Now, think of ways to use your *singing* voice to describe John's ghost.

The Ghost of John

WORDS AND MUSIC BY MARTHA GRUBB

"POOR TOM" FROM ROUNDS. USED THROUGH COURTESY OF COOPERATIVE RECREATION SERVICE, INC., DELAWARE, OHIO.

Have you seen the ghost of John?

Long white bones with the skin all gone,_____

Oo,   Oo,_____

Would-n't it be chil - ly with no skin on!

How does the composer use dynamics in this piece for orchestra?

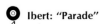
Ibert: "Parade"

FOLLOW THE SIGNS

Play one of these parts on a ringing instrument to accompany "The Ghost of John."

Which sign tells you to get louder? Get softer? Get louder then softer?

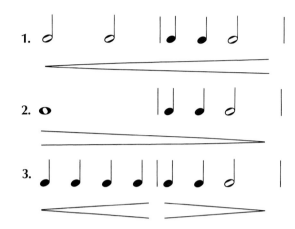

Notice that two quarter notes can take the place of a half note.

How many quarter notes can take the place of a whole note?

How many half notes can take the place of a whole note?

NEW NOTE—D

Low D

Parts for "The Ghost of John"

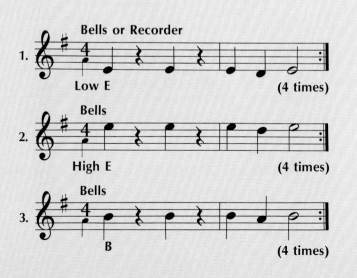

1. Bells or Recorder
Low E   (4 times)

2. Bells
High E   (4 times)

3. Bells
B   (4 times)

DYNAMICS HELP TELL A STORY

Listen to "In the Hall of the Mountain King."
You will hear one little tune repeated over and over.
How did the composer use dynamics and tempo to
make the music more and more exciting?

◎ Grieg: "In the Hall of the Mountain King"
4

CALL CHART 2: *Dynamics* ◎
4

In this piece you will hear many changes of dynamics.
Follow the chart as you listen. It will help you hear
what is going on as the music moves along.

1.	LOUD
2.	SOFT
3.	LOUD
4.	GETTING SOFTER
5.	GETTING LOUDER
6.	LOUD

Locke: *Saraband*

TWO SONGS IN DIFFERENT STYLES

Polly Wolly Doodle
AMERICAN FOLK SONG

1. Oh, I went down South for to see my Sal,
2. Oh, my Sal, she is a____ maid - en fair,

Sing - ing Pol - ly Wol - ly Doo - dle all the day;
Sing - ing Pol - ly Wol - ly Doo - dle all the day;

My____ Sal, she is a____ spunk - y gal,
With____ curl - y eyes and____ laugh - ing hair,

Sing - ing Pol - ly Wol - ly Doo - dle all the day.
Sing - ing Pol - ly Wol - ly Doo - dle all the day.

REFRAIN

Fare thee well,____ fare thee well,____ Fare thee well my fair - y fay,____

For I'm goin' to Loui - si - an - a, For to see my Su - sy - an - na,

Sing - ing Pol - ly Wol - ly Doo - dle all the day.____

74

3. The partridge is a pretty bird,

   It has a speckled breast,

   It steals away the farmer's grain,

   And totes it to its nest! *Refrain*

4. The raccoon's tail is ringed around,

   The 'possum's tail is bare,

   The rabbit's got no tail at all,

   Just a little bitty bunch of hair! *Refrain*

Shepherd, Shepherd

BLACK SPIRITUAL

FROM AMERICAN NEGRO SONGS AND SPIRITUALS BY JOHN W. WORK. COPYRIGHT © 1940, 1968 BY CROWN PUBLISHERS, INC.
REPRINTED BY PERMISSION OF CROWN PUBLISHERS, INC.

Will your voice be loud, or soft, when you sing

"Shepherd, Shepherd"?

1. Shep - herd, Shep - herd, where'd you lose your sheep?
2. Shep - herd, Shep - herd, where'd you leave your lambs?

Shep - herd, Shep - herd, where'd you lose your sheep?
Shep - herd, Shep - herd, where'd you leave your lambs?

Shep - herd, Shep - herd, where'd you lose your sheep?
Shep - herd, Shep - herd, where'd you leave your lambs?

O the sheep all gone a - stray,___
O the sheep all gone a - stray,___

The sheep all gone___ a - stray.
The sheep all gone___ a - stray.

Listen for the dynamics in two pieces for orchestra.

Are they the same in each piece, or different?

Shostakovich: "Polka"

Mendelssohn: "Nocturne"

75

SOUND PIECE 2: *Dynamic Design*

DAVID S. WALKER

This sound piece uses two different ways to show dynamics—an old way and a new way. Can you tell which is which?

Notice when you play loud and soft in Idea A.

Idea A

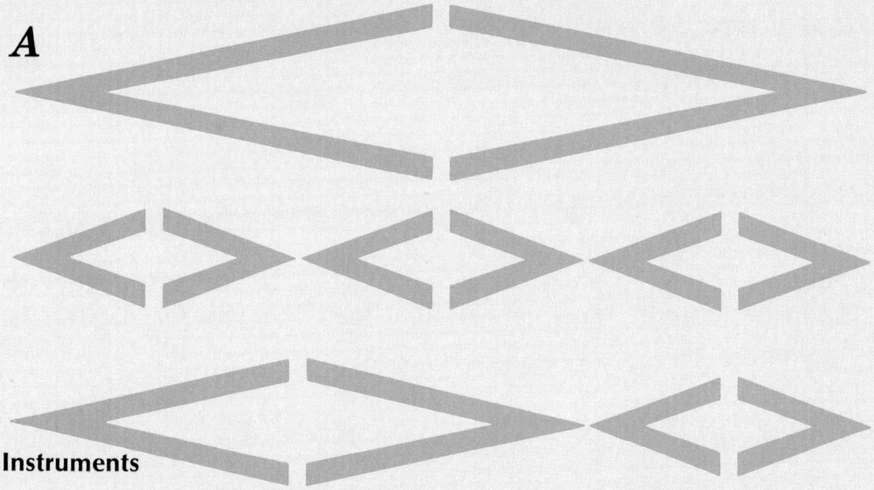

Ringing Instruments

Can you discover how to play one of the instruments in Idea B? Follow the color line. It will tell you when to play louder or softer.

Idea B

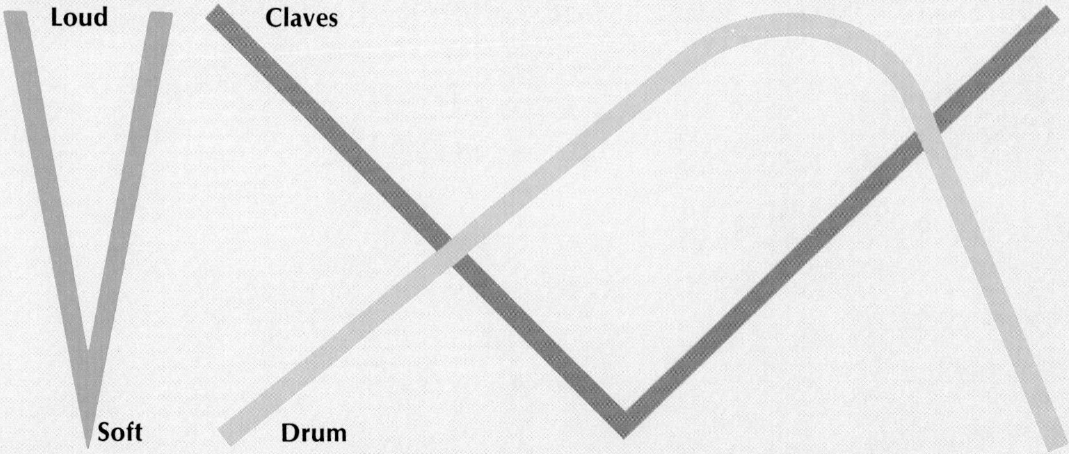
Loud
Claves
Soft
Drum

Play your part of the sound piece alone before playing it with others.

Make up your own sound piece using some of these ideas.

LOUD, OR SOFT?

Do you think this song should be sung loud, or soft?
Smooth, or bouncy? Why?

What You Gonna Call Your Pretty Little Baby?

BLACK SPIRITUAL

REFRAIN

What you gon - na call your pret - ty lit - tle ba - by,

What you gon - na call your pret - ty lit - tle ba - by,

What you gon - na call your pret - ty lit - tle ba - by,

Fine

Born, born in Beth - le - hem?____

1. Some say one thing, I'll say Im - man - uel,

D.C.

Born, born in Beth - le - hem.____

2. Some call Him one thing,
   I'll call Him Jesus,
   Born, born in Bethlehem.

3. Sweet little baby,
   Born in a manger,
   Born, born in Bethlehem.

PLAN YOUR OWN DYNAMICS

Pray God Bless

ROUND FROM ENGLAND

Pray God bless all friends here,

A mer-ry, mer-ry Christ-mas and a hap-py New Year.

Choose one of these parts to play on bells or recorder.

Play the part all through "Pray God Bless."

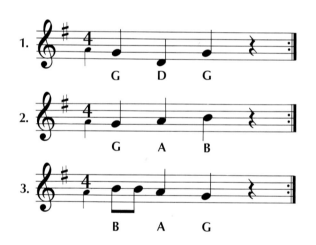

1. G D G

2. G A B

3. B A G

Valentine Round

WORDS ANONYMOUS   MUSIC BY DAVID EDDLEMAN

Do you love me, or do___ you___ not?

You told me once___ but___ I for-got!

78

WHAT DO YOU HEAR? 4: *Dynamics* 🔘
4

Each time a number is called, decide what dynamics you hear and draw a circle around the correct word.

Listen. Then circle what you hear.

Locke: *Saraband*

1. LOUD   SOFT

2. LOUD   SOFT

3. LOUD   SOFT

4. GETTING LOUDER   GETTING SOFTER

5. GETTING LOUDER   GETTING SOFTER

6. LOUD   SOFT

Style: **American Indian**

To accompany the singing and
dancing, Indians use drums and
rattles.

Each drum and rattle has a design of
its own.

Through these designs, Indians show
their feelings for things in nature.

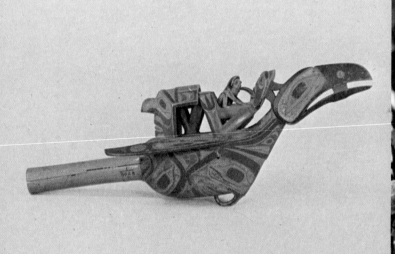

In all styles of Indian music, the voice is the most important instrument.

The singers follow a song leader, who sets the tempo and decides how high or how low they will sing.

Listen to the accompaniment of these Indian songs. Which ones use rattles? Which ones use drums?

Navajo Night Chant

Sioux Rabbit Dance

Stomp Dance

You heard a special way of singing and playing found in much Indian music.
When you listen again, notice some other things to be found in the music of American Indians.

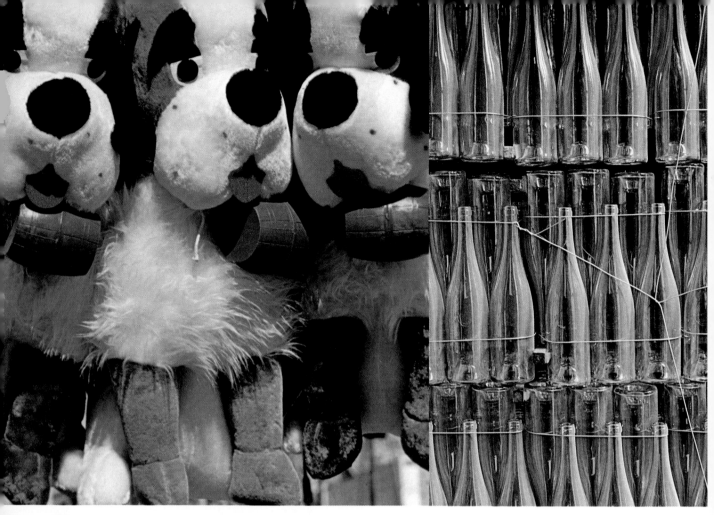

Form: *Repetition, Contrast*

Oh, What a Beautiful City

BLACK SPIRITUAL

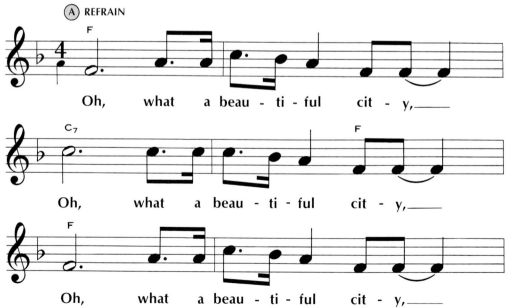

Ⓐ REFRAIN

Oh, what a beau - ti - ful cit - y, _____

Oh, what a beau - ti - ful cit - y, _____

Oh, what a beau - ti - ful cit - y, _____

Twelve gates - a to the cit-y,___ Hal - le - lu - jah!

B VERSE

Three gates ___ to the East,

Three gates ___ to the West,

Three gates ___ to the North,___

Three gates ___ to the South,

There's twelve gates - a to the cit-y,___ Hal - le - lu - jah!

CONTRAST GAME

Think of a word that might fit in each blank.

Music can be loud; music can be _____.

Music can be high; music can be _____.

Music can be fast; music can be _____.

Notes can be long; notes can be _____.

Notes can move upward; notes can move _____.

TWO DIFFERENT SECTIONS

You can show two different sections in music by doing a dance to "Boil Them Cabbage Down." Look at the pictures. What is happening in section A? In section B?

Do you find accent marks (>) in section A, or in section B? What do the accent marks tell you?

Boil Them Cabbage Down

AMERICAN PIONEER SONG

FROM MORE SONGS OF THE NEW WORLD BY DESMOND MacMAHON, PUBLISHED BY HOLMES McDOUGALL LIMITED

A VERSE

1. The rac-coon's got a fur-ry tail,
The pos-sum's tail is bare,—
The rab-bit ain't got no tail at all,
But a lit-tle bit o' bunch o' hair.

B REFRAIN

Boil them cab-bage down, down, Bake them bis-cuits brown, brown,
The on-ly tune I ev-er did learn is Boil them cab-bage down.

2. The June bug he has wings of gold,
   The firefly wings of flame,
   The bedbug's got no wings at all,
   But he gets there just the same. *Refrain*

3. Oh, love it is a killing fit
   When beauty hits a blossom,
   And if you want your finger bit,
   Just poke it at a possum. *Refrain*

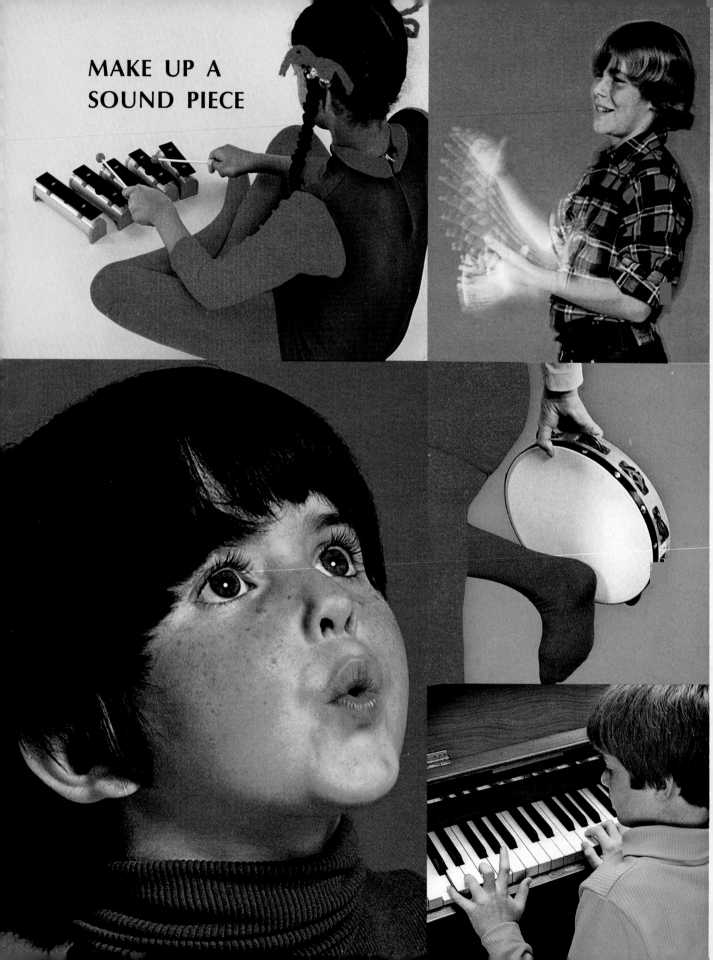

MAKE UP A
SOUND PIECE

This sound piece was written especially for you. You will find a picture of the composer, Doris Hays, on page 58 in your book.

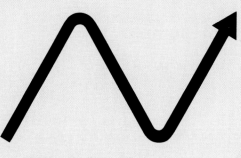

Play on bells or piano

Start

A

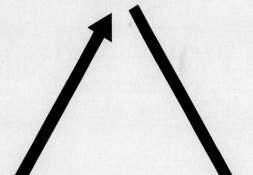

Start

Hand sounds

Foot sounds   Mouth sounds

B

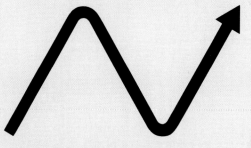

Play on bells or piano

Start

A

What makes the contrast in this sound piece? Make up your own sound piece using some of these ideas.

CIRCLES AND SQUARES

Shapes and letters can show form in music.

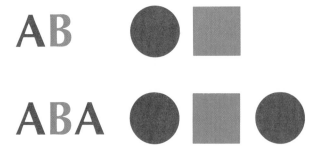

Which set of shapes and letters shows the form of
"Little David, Play on Your Harp"? To help you answer
the question, listen to the recording.

Little David, Play on Your Harp

BLACK SPIRITUAL

Lit-tle Da-vid, play on your harp, Hal - le - lu, hal - le - lu,

Fine

Lit-tle Da-vid, play on your harp, Hal - le - lu.

Lit-tle Da - vid was a shep-herd boy,_____

D.C. al Fine

He killed Go - li - ath and shout-ed for joy.

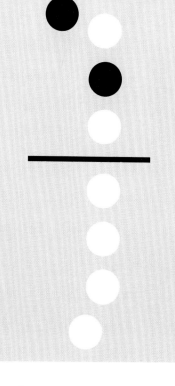

NEW NOTE—HIGH C

High C

Play one of these parts
throughout section A
of "Little David,
Play on Your Harp."

Now try a
countermelody
for "Ain't Gonna Rain,"
page 24.

Oh, Won't You Sit Down?

BLACK SPIRITUAL

CALL CHART 3: *Form* 🎯4

Listen for different sections in this piece for orchestra. The chart will help you hear the form.

Tchaikovsky: "Trepak"

1.	*A*
2.	*A (REPETITION)*
3.	*B (CONTRAST)*
4.	*A (REPETITION)*

CALL CHART 4: *Form* 🎯4

Listen for different sections in this piece. You will hear brass instruments only. The chart will help you hear the form.

Purcell: *Trumpet Tune*

1.	*A*
2.	*A (REPETITION)*
3.	*B (CONTRAST)*
4.	*B (CONTRAST)*

A SONG IN TWO SECTIONS

Which section has meter in 3?

Which section has meter in 2?

Find two different ways to play a tambourine. Play the tambourine one way for section A. Play a different way for section B.

Piñata Song

CHRISTMAS SONG FROM MEXICO   ENGLISH WORDS BY VERNE MUNOZ

In the hap - py days of Christ - mas,_____

Sounds of glad - ness fill the air;_____

When it's time for the pi - ña - ta,_____

There's ex - cite - ment ev - 'ry - where._____

Take a stick and whack it, Be the one to crack it;

Win pi - ña - ta's trea - sure, Can - dies for your plea - sure.

WHAT DO YOU HEAR? 5: *Form* 🎵

When the music starts and the voice on the recording says "one," you are hearing section A, as shown on the chart.

At each number that follows, decide whether the section is a *repetition* of A or a *contrast* of A.

1.	A	
2.	REPETITION	CONTRAST
3.	REPETITION	CONTRAST
4.	REPETITION	CONTRAST
5.	REPETITION	CONTRAST

Giuliani: *Grand Sonata in A Major for Flute and Guitar,* "Scherzo" (excerpt)

1.	A	
2.	REPETITION	CONTRAST
3.	REPETITION	CONTRAST
4.	REPETITION	CONTRAST

Pinto: "Run Run"

The Arts: Repetition/Contrast

Can you find repetition and contrast in this painting?

Can you find repetition and contrast in this poem?

BUT YOU ARE MINE

Someone would like to have you for her child

but you are mine.

Someone would like to rear you on a costly mat

but you are mine.

Someone would like to place you on a camel blanket

but you are mine.

I have you to rear on a torn old mat.

Someone would like to have you as her child

but you are mine.

—From Africa

O'Keeffe: *The White Canadian Barn, No. 2*

Now say the poem to find the ideas that contrast.

There is repetition and contrast in music and painting and poetry.

Each art uses repetition and contrast in its own way.

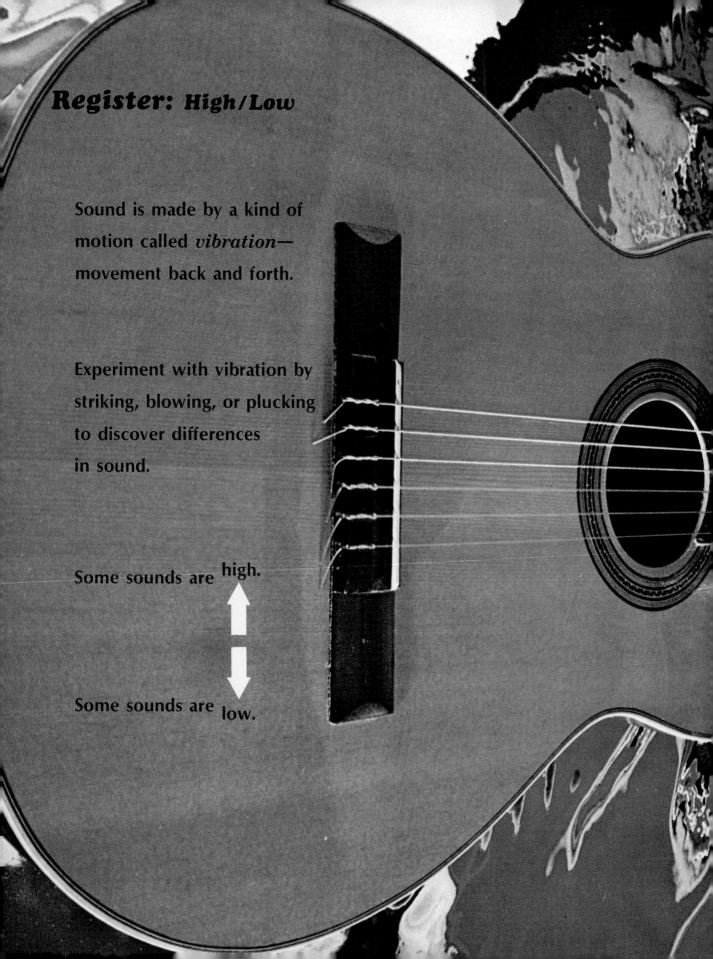

Register: *High/Low*

Sound is made by a kind of
motion called *vibration*—
movement back and forth.

Experiment with vibration by
striking, blowing, or plucking
to discover differences
in sound.

Some sounds are high.

Some sounds are low.

Which sounds higher?

Why?

Which sounds higher?

Why?

Which sounds higher?

Why?

97

A LEAP FROM HIGH TO LOW

The Sow Took the Measles

AMERICAN FRONTIER SONG

How do you think I be-gan in the world?

I got me a sow and sev-'ral oth-er thing.

The sow took the mea-sles and she died in the spring.

1. What do you think I made of her hide?

The ver-y best sad-dle that you ev-er did ride.

Sad-dle or bri-dle or an-y such thing,

D.C. after verse 4

The sow took the mea-sles and she died in the spring.

2. What do you think I made of her nose?

The very best thimble that ever sewed clothes.

Thimble or thread or any such thing,

The sow took the measles and she died in the spring.

98

3. What do you think I made of her tail?

   The very best whup that ever sought sail.

   Whup or whupsocket or any such thing,

   The sow took the measles and she died in the spring.

4. What do you think I made of her feet?

   The very best pickles that you ever did eat.

   Pickles or glue or any such thing,

   The sow took the measles and she died in the spring. *Refrain*

Find two C bells, one low and one high. Play one of these bell parts over and over while others sing "The Sow Took the Measles."

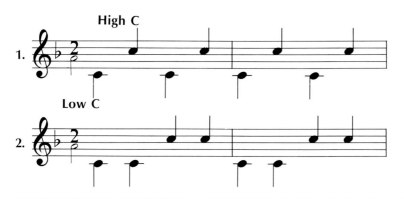

CALL CHART 5: *Register*

The Call Chart will help you hear when the music is mostly low, mostly high, and both low and high.

1.	*MOSTLY LOW*
2.	*MOSTLY HIGH*
3.	*BOTH LOW AND HIGH*
4.	*MOSTLY LOW*

Mussorgsky: *Pictures at an Exhibition,* "Samuel Goldenberg and Schmuyle"

A LOW-HIGH-HIGH PATTERN

Find a space in the room to walk a low-high-high pattern. While some children move, take turns playing one of the instruments to accompany them.

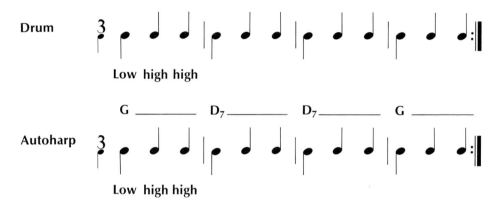

Drum

Low high high

Autoharp

G _____ D₇ _____ D₇ _____ G _____

Low high high

To play a recorder part for "Bella Bimba," you need low D and a new note, high D.

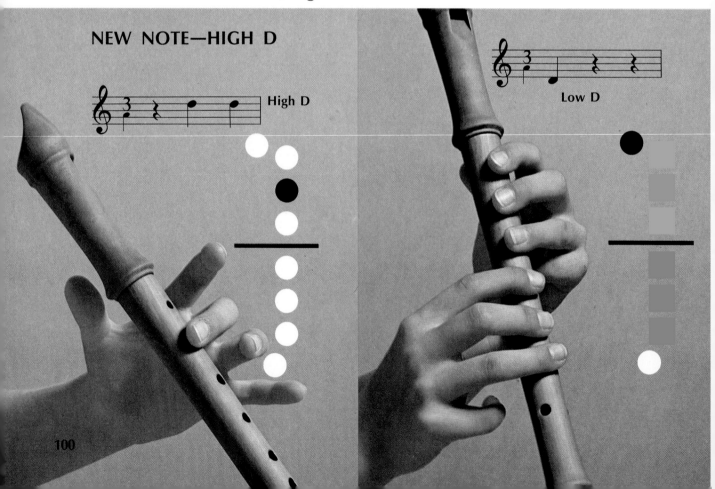

NEW NOTE—HIGH D

High D

Low D

THINGS TO DO WITH "BELLA BIMBA"

During section A of "Bella Bimba" you can

· Walk a low-high-high pattern

· Play a low-high-high pattern on an instrument—
drum, Autoharp, or recorder.

Bella Bimba

FOLK SONG FROM ITALY   ENGLISH WORDS BY RICHARD MORRIS

How well you dance, my *bel - la bim - ba,* *bel - la*

bim - ba, bel - la bim - ba. How well you dance, my *bel - la*

bim - ba, bel - la bim - ba, how you dance!

1. Bright as a sun - beam, Grace - ful and fair,___

Light as a feath - er, Float - ing on air.

2. Whirling and twirling,

    Round and around,

    Feet always moving

    When music sounds.

For more things to do with "Bella Bimba," turn the page.

MORE THINGS TO DO WITH "BELLA BIMBA"

You have played high and low sounds on a drum, on the strings of an Autoharp, or on a recorder.

Now play a bell part to accompany section A of "Bella Bimba."

Call the lower note "one" and count all the lines and spaces to the higher note. It will be "eight." The two notes are an *octave* apart.

Now play the notes, *octave* D, at the same time to discover that they sound alike.

Find other bells that sound the same when played together.

Your ears will tell you when you are playing octaves.

Play octaves to accompany "Bella Bimba."

Play octave D during section A.

Play octave B during section B.

Make up your own rhythm pattern.

102

WHAT DO YOU HEAR? 6: *Register* 🔘

Each time a number is called, decide whether the music is mostly high or mostly low.

If you think it is mostly high, circle the words **MOSTLY HIGH.**
If you think it is mostly low, circle the words **MOSTLY LOW.**
Listen. Then circle what you hear.

1	MOSTLY HIGH	MOSTLY LOW
2	MOSTLY HIGH	MOSTLY LOW
3	MOSTLY HIGH	MOSTLY LOW
4	MOSTLY HIGH	MOSTLY LOW
5	MOSTLY HIGH	MOSTLY LOW
6	MOSTLY HIGH	MOSTLY LOW

Haydn: *Symphony No. 103,* "Adagio"

1	MOSTLY HIGH	MOSTLY LOW
2	MOSTLY HIGH	MOSTLY LOW
3	MOSTLY HIGH	MOSTLY LOW

Grieg: "In the Hall of the Mountain King"
Beethoven: *Symphony No. 7,* Movement 4
Britten: *The Young Person's Guide to the Orchestra*

SING-A-STORY

Will you say the spoken parts in a high, or a low voice?

Will you say the parts loud, or soft?

One Day My Mother Went to the Market

FOLK SONG FROM ITALY   ENGLISH WORDS BY LEO ISRAEL   COLLECTED AND ADAPTED BY RUDOLPH GOEHR

1. One day my moth-er went to the mar-ket

And she bought a hand-some roost-er.

A roost-er?   A roost-er!

But when my moth-er start-ed to cook him,

He did ev'-ry-thing he use-ta.

He use-ta?   He use-ta!

Oh, he said, "Cock-a-doo-dle-doo,

How I love you, how I love you."

Oh, he said, "Cock - a doo - dle - doo,"

And a - way he flew, and a - way he flew.

2. . . . and she bought a little pig . . .

But when my mother started to cook him,

He got up and danced a jig . . .

Oh, he said, "Oink, oink, oink,

Though I'd like to stay, though I'd like to stay."

Oh, he said, "Oink, oink, oink,"

And he ran away, and he ran away.

3. . . . and she bought a pretty lamb . . .

But when my mother started to cook him,

He said, "Who do you think I am?" . . .

Oh, he said, "Baa, baa, baa,

I'm silly, it's true, I'm silly, it's true."

Oh, he said, "Baa, baa, baa,

Not as silly as you, not as silly as you."

4. . . . and she bought a lovely hen . . .

But when my mother started to cook her,

She began to cluck again . . .

Oh, she said, "Cluck, cluck, cluck, cluck, cluck."

But she forgot, but she forgot,

Oh, she said, "Cluck, cluck, cluck, cluck, cluck,"

And fell into the pot, and fell into the pot.

Style: *Two Different Styles*

Look at the symbols on these pages. They tell you something about the *qualities* of music.

As you listen to the first piece, look at the symbols in the left-hand column. When you listen to the second piece, look at the symbols in the right-hand column. Each piece has a different style.

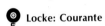 Locke: Courante  Brahms: Hungarian Dance No. 6

Beat steady

Beat changes

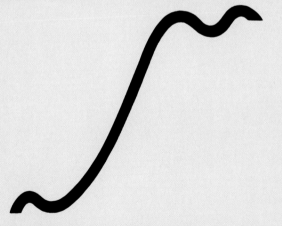

Register very high and very low

Register not very high or very low

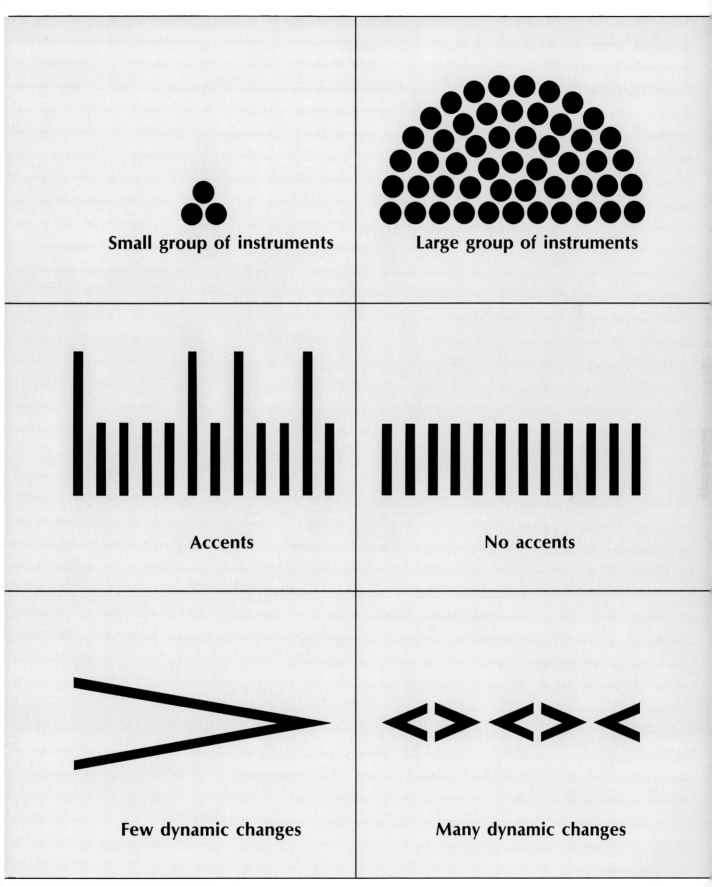

Small group of instruments

Large group of instruments

Accents

No accents

Few dynamic changes

Many dynamic changes

Duration:
Long, Short

Make long sounds and short sounds with your voice.

5 BLUM

Dog means dog,
And cat means cat;
And there are lots
Of words like that.
A cart's a cart
To pull or shove,
A plate's a plate,
To eat off of.
But there are other
Words I say
When I am left
Alone to play.
Blum is one.
Blum is a word
That very few
Have ever heard.
I like to say it.
"Blum, Blum, Blum"—
I do it loud
Or in a hum.
All by itself
It's nice to sing:
It does not mean
A single thing.

Dorothy Aldis

What Is Love?

WORDS AND MUSIC BY CHRIS DEDRICK © 1972 ALMITRA MUSIC COMPANY, INC.

Follow the notes as you listen to the recording. Do the notes in the color boxes show long sounds or short sounds?

I know a ver-y hard ques-tion: What is love?

Ver-y wise peo-ple can't find the words to say what love is.

I fig-ured out that there can't be words for some-thing quite that good.

If you stop, If you stop to think a-bout your friends, your folks,

Your pup-py, your cat, the sun-shine, the trees and e-ven your-self—

You know all a-bout love; Al-most ev-'ry-one does.

Love, love, I know all a-bout love, but I can't tell.

Love, love, Words can't tell a-bout love, it's just as well.

HOW TO WRITE LONG AND SHORT SOUNDS

Find these notes in the song on page 109.

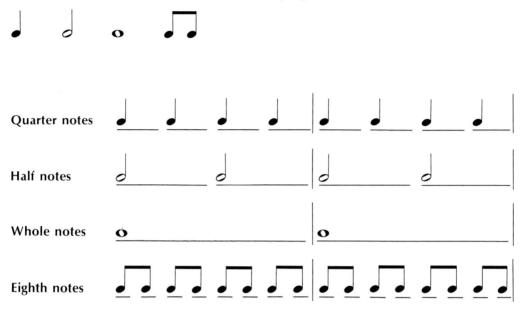

How many quarter notes can take the place of a half note?

How many eighth notes can take the place of a half note?

How many eighth notes can take the place of a quarter note?

How many quarter notes can take the place of a whole note?

Long and short sounds can make a rhythm pattern.

Find these patterns in the music on page 109.

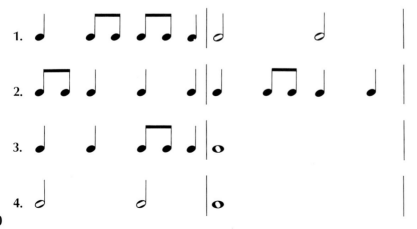

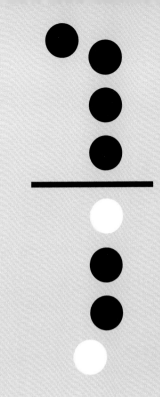

NEW NOTE—F♯

Play this pattern when it comes in the song "What Is Love?"

Love,   love,

CALL CHART 6: *Duration* ⊚₅

Can you hear long and short sounds in a piano piece?

Listen to the recording and check the chart to help you.

Chopin: *Scherzo No. 3 in C♯ Minor*

1. LONG SOUNDS	4. SHORT SOUNDS
2. SHORT SOUNDS	5. LONG SOUNDS
3. LONG SOUNDS	6. SHORT SOUNDS
	7. LONG SOUNDS

ECHO GAME

How good are your ears? You will hear six rhythm patterns on the recording. In the pause after each pattern, echo what you hear.

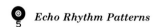 *Echo Rhythm Patterns*

Sing this song about the old dog Blue as though you were telling a story.

Old Blue SOUTHERN MOUNTAIN SONG

VERSE
1. I had an old dog,

And his name was Blue,

And I bet-cha five dol-lars he's a good dog, too.

REFRAIN
Come on, Blue, you good dog, you;

Come on, Blue, you good dog, you.

2. I grabbed my axe and I tooted my horn,
   Gonna git me a 'possum in the new-ground corn. *Refrain*

3. Chased that ol' 'possum up a 'simmon tree,
   Blue looked at the 'possum, 'possum looked at me. *Refrain*

4. Blue grinned at me, I grinned at him,
   I shook out the 'possum, Blue took him in. *Refrain*

5. Baked that 'possum all good and brown,
   And I laid them sweet potatoes 'round and 'round. *Refrain*

6. Well, old Blue died, and he died so hard,
   That he shook the ground in my back yard. *Refrain*

7. I dug his grave with a silver spade,
   I let him down with a golden chain. *Refrain*

8. When I get to heaven, first thing I'll do,
   Grab me a horn and blow for old Blue. *Refrain*

Find the places in "Old Blue" where you sing a long sound. They are shown in the color boxes.

Clap a pattern of shorter sounds each time you sing one of the long sounds.

Listen to two pieces for instruments. The pieces are in different styles, but in each piece you will hear short and long sounds played at the same time.

Vivaldi: *The Four Seasons* (Winter)

Baldridge: *Let's Dance*

A RHYTHM PATTERN THAT REPEATS

The Pig

FOLK TUNE FROM MEXICO   ENGLISH WORDS BY MARGARET MARKS

Mis - sus Tor - res had a pi - hig,

Ver - y fat and ver - y bi - hig,

Dressed him in a fun - ny wi - hig,

Tried to make him dance a ji - hig.

But the pig, whose name was Sa - ham,

Said, "I'm ver - y sor - ry, Ma - ham,

Can't you leave me as I a - ham?

I don't want to be a ha - ham!"

AFRICAN RHYTHM COMPLEX

Chant the numbers in each line. Clap each time you say a large-size number.

1 2 3 4 5 6 7 8 9 10 11 12

1 2 3 4 5 6 7 8 9 10 11 12

1 2 3 4 5 6 7 8 9 10 11 12

Look at the notation for the rhythms you clapped.

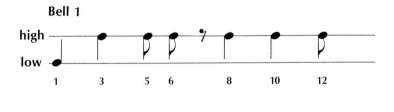

Bell 1

high
low

1   3   5 6   8   10   12

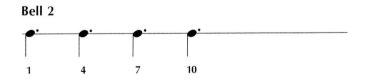

Bell 2

1   4   7   10

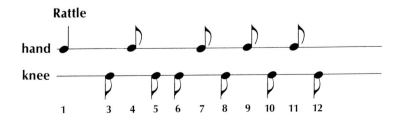

Rattle

hand
knee

1   3 4 5 6 7 8 9 10 11 12

SOUND AND SILENCE

Sound and silence can work together in a rhythm pattern.

In music, sounds are shown with notes; silences with rests.

Scratch, Scratch

WORDS AND MUSIC BY HARRY BELAFONTE AND LORD BURGESS

1. Oh, we went out to a par-ty,

It was me and Ben and Mac,

And be-fore I knew what hap-pened,

I got an itch-in' on my back.

REFRAIN

Scratch, scratch me back,   Scratch, scratch me back.

It real-ly is a fact,____

The less I itch,   the more I scratch.

2. Well, I was quite embarrassed,
   Till my two friends I did see,
   Well, they were madly itching,
   And they were screaming louder than me.
   Refrain

3. Now, this scratching was contagious,
   And it didn't take very long,
   Ev'rybody there was itching,
   As they joined me in this song.
   Refrain

Rabbit Hash

PATTING CHANT
6

COLLECTED, ADAPTED AND ARRANGED BY JOHN A. LOMAX & ALAN LOMAX   TRO—© COPYRIGHT 1934 AND RENEWED 1962 LUDLOW MUSIC, INC., NEW YORK, N.Y. USED BY PERMISSION

**Keep time to the steady beat as you say this
patting chant.
Notice how sound and silence work together.**

Oh, rab-bit, rab-bit, rab-bit, rab-bit a-hash,

An' pole-cat smash.

Rab-bit, rab-bit, rab-bit a-hash.

Rab-bit skip, an' rab-bit hop, An' rab-bit eat my tur-nip top.

Oh, rab-bit, rab-bit, rab-bit a-hash!

Oh, rab-bit a-hash!

THREE DIFFERENT RHYTHM PATTERNS

Each pattern is shown in a different colored box. Listen for other places in the song that match the patterns in the color boxes.

The Barnyard

WORDS AND MUSIC BY CARMINO RAVOSA

© 1972 CARMINO RAVOSA

1. Barn - yard, barn - yard, all a-round the barn - yard,

Hear the cow go, "Moo, moo."

Barn - yard, barn - yard, all a-round the barn - yard,

Hear the duck go, "Quack, quack."

All a-round the barn-yard, An - i-mals are talk - ing;

Though it sounds to you like Just a lot of squawk-ing.

Barn - yard, barn - yard, all a-round the barn - yard,

Hear the goose go, "Honk, honk."

Barn - yard, barn - yard, all a-round the barn - yard,

Hear the chick-en, "Cluck, cluck, Cluck, cluck."

2. Barnyard, barnyard, all around the barnyard,

Hear the pig go, "Oink, oink."

Barnyard, barnyard, all around the barnyard,

Hear the sheep go, "Baa, baa."

All around the barnyard,

Animals are talking;

Though it sounds to you like

Just a lot of squawking.

Barnyard, barnyard, all around the barnyard,

Hear the horse go, "Neigh, neigh."

Barnyard, barnyard, all around the barnyard,

Hear the donkey, "Hee-haw, Hee-haw."

Play an accent on a percussion instrument before each animal sound.

Moo, moo   Quack, quack   Honk, honk

Listen for accents in this piece for piano.

Bartók: *Roumanian Dance No. 6*

ACCENTS

In music, a sudden loud sound is called an *accent*.

Find the sign (>) that shows accent in this song.

Follow the notes as you listen to the recording. Clap on all the accents.

Play the accents on a small drum or on finger cymbals.

Shepherds Came to Bethlehem
POLISH CAROL

ENGLISH WORDS BY ROSEMARY JACQUES

1. Shep-herds came to Beth - le - hem on Christ - mas Day.

How the Ba - by smiled as they their pipes did play.

Glo - ry, sing glo - ry to God in the high - est,

And peace on earth, Peace on earth.

2. Then a shepherd beat upon a little drum.

   How it pleased the Baby with its rum-tum-tum.

   Glory, . . .

3. As the shepherds bowed before the blessed Boy,

   All the heavens rang with sounds of wondrous joy.

   Glory, . . .

120

ADD A PART

Practice one of these instrumental parts, then play it to accompany "Shepherds Came to Bethlehem."

WHAT DO YOU HEAR? 7: *Duration* 🔵

What do you hear? Each time a number is called,
decide whether you hear mostly short sounds, mostly
long sounds, or short and long sounds played together.

Listen. Then circle what you hear.

---

1. SHORT SOUNDS   LONG SOUNDS

SHORT AND LONG SOUNDS TOGETHER

---

2. SHORT SOUNDS   LONG SOUNDS

SHORT AND LONG SOUNDS TOGETHER

---

3. SHORT SOUNDS   LONG SOUNDS

SHORT AND LONG SOUNDS TOGETHER

---

4. SHORT SOUNDS   LONG SOUNDS

SHORT AND LONG SOUNDS TOGETHER

Hays: *Sound Piece 3*
Vivaldi: *The Four Seasons* (Winter)
Ebreo: *Falla con misuras*
Mama Paquita

WHAT DO YOU HEAR? 8: *Rhythm Patterns*

What do you hear? As each number is called, look at the notation and circle the rhythm pattern you hear.

1

2

3

4

The Lily Bud
Mozart: *Symphony No. 40*
The Pig
Bach: *Passacaglia in C Minor*

123

Slatter: Sampler

Tone Color

You can use your voice to make different tone colors.

Find words that imitate sounds in this poem.

When you say the poem, make your voice imitate the sounds.

LEWIS HAS A TRUMPET

A trumpet
A trumpet
Lewis has a trumpet
A bright one that's yellow
A loud proud horn.
He blows it in the evening
When the moon is newly rising
He blows it when it's raining
In the cold and misty morn
It honks and it whistles
It roars like a lion
It rumbles like a lion
With a wheezy huffing hum
His parents say it's awful
Oh really simply awful
But
Lewis says he loves it
It's such a handsome trumpet
And when he's through with trumpets
He's going to buy a drum.

Karla Kuskin

 *Hammer Ring*   *Vocal Tone Colors*

126

The recorder has its own tone color.
When you play a recorder, you make
the sound by blowing.
All instruments that are played by
blowing are called *wind instruments.*
How many do you know?

French horn

clarinet

recorder

trumpet and trombone

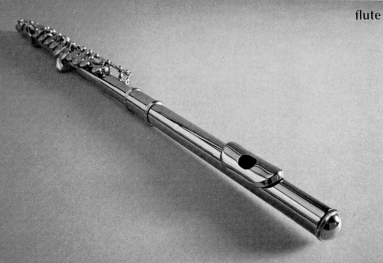

flute

Do you know
wind instruments
by their tone color?
Point to the picture
that shows what
you hear on the recording.

 Tone Colors of Wind Instruments

127

THE SOUND OF RECORDERS

The songs on pages 128 and 129 can be played on the recorder. They use notes that you have learned so far.

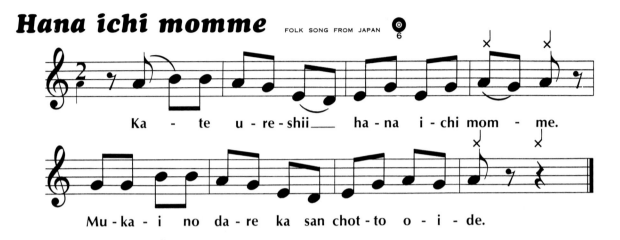

Hana ichi momme   FOLK SONG FROM JAPAN

Ka - te u - re - shii___ ha - na i - chi mom - me.

Mu - ka - i no da - re ka san chot - to o - i - de.

Here is another recorder part to play with the melody of "Hana ichi momme." This part is called a *countermelody*.

Recorder

E   D   A   G

Add one of these bell parts to the melody.

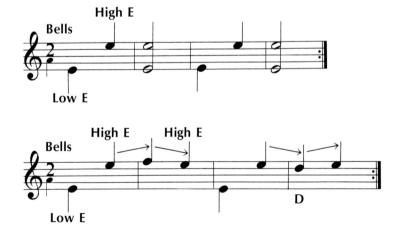

Bells
High E
Low E

Bells
High E   High E
Low E   D

Add the sound of the woodblock when it comes in the song.

Imagination of Grand Sea

FOLK SONG FROM JAPAN

ENGLISH WORDS BY RICHARD MORRIS

To add another tone color to this song, play finger cymbals on the first beat of every measure.

U - mi wa hi - ro - i na oh - ki - i na,

Tsu - ki ga no - bo - ru shi hi ga shi - zu - mu.

1. Grand is the evening sea, majestic and deep;
   There, as the moon awakes, the sun will go to sleep.

2. Calm are the mighty waves; the water, so blue;
   I wonder where the sea and all the waves go to.

3. Many the tiny ships that float on the sea;
   Some day to foreign lands those ships will carry me.

Ay, Di, Di, Di

HASIDIC MELODY

Ay, di, di, di, ay, di, di, di, di;

Ay, di, di, di, di, ay, di, di, di, di.

Play this bell part all through the song.

Bells

D   G

THE SOUND OF PERCUSSION

Yankee Doodle

TRADITIONAL   WORDS BY DR. RICHARD SHUCKBURGH

1. 7 Fath'r and I went down to camp,
2. And there we saw a thou - sand men,

A - long with Cap - tain Good - in',
As rich as Squire_____ Da - vid;

And there we saw the men and boys
And what they wast - ed ev - 'ry day,

As thick as hast y pud - din'.
I wish it could be sav - ed.

REFRAIN

Yan - kee Doo - dle, keep it up, Yan - kee Doo - dle dan - dy,

Mind the mu - sic and the step And with the girls be hand - y.

3. And there was Captain Washington
   Upon a slapping stallion,
   A-giving orders to his men;
   I guess there was a million.

Drum

Cymbals

130

Battle Hymn of the Republic

MUSIC BY WILLIAM STEFFE

WORDS BY JULIA WARD HOWE

Glo - ry, glo - ry, hal - le - lu - jah!

Glo - ry, glo - ry, hal - le - lu - jah!

Glo - ry, glo - ry, hal - le - lu - jah! His truth is march-ing on.

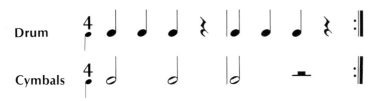

Drum

Cymbals

Jingle Bells

WORDS AND MUSIC BY JAMES PIERPONT

Jin - gle bells, jin - gle bells, jin - gle all the way!

Oh, what fun it is to ride in a one-horse o - pen sleigh! _____

Jin - gle bells, jin - gle bells, jin - gle all the way!

Oh, what fun it is to ride in a one-horse o - pen sleigh!

THE SOUND OF THE AUTOHARP

You can accompany the songs on pages 132 and 133 on the Autoharp. The chord letters above the music will tell you when to change from one chord to another.

For Health and Strength

OLD ENGLISH ROUND

For health and strength and dai - ly food We praise Thy name, O Lord.

Frère Jacques

FRENCH ROUND

Frè - re Jac - ques, Frè - re Jac - ques,

Dor - mez - vous, Dor - mez - vous?

Son - nez les ma - ti - nes, Son - nez les ma - ti - nes,

Din din don, Din din don.

Oh, Susanna

WORDS AND MUSIC BY STEPHEN FOSTER

I___ came from Al - a - ba - ma With my ban - jo on my knee,

I'm___ going to Loui - si - an - a, My___ true love for to see;

It___ rained all night the day I left, The weath-er it was dry;

The__ sun so hot I froze to death; Su - san - na, don't you cry.

REFRAIN

Oh, Su - san - na, Oh, don't you cry for me,

I've__ come from Al - a - ba - ma With my ban - jo on my knee.

2. I had a dream the other night,

When ev'rything was still.

I thought I saw Susanna

A-coming down the hill.

The buckwheat cake was in her mouth,

The tear was in her eye.

Says I, "I'm coming from the South,

Susanna, don't you cry." *Refrain*

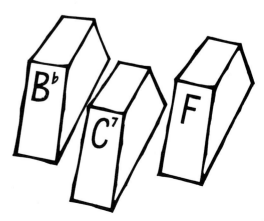

HOW GOOD ARE YOUR EARS?

Listen to the recording of "Nobody's Business." What instruments accompany the song?

Nobody's Business

AMERICAN FOLK SONG

FROM PLAY-PARTY GAMES OF PIONEER TIMES, PUBLISHED BY COOPERATIVE RECREATION SERVICE, INC. USED BY PERMISSION.

VERSE

1. I went to town in a lit-tle red wag-on,

Come back home with the hub a-drag-gin',

It's no-bod-y's busi-ness what I do.

REFRAIN

It's no-bod-y's busi-ness, busi-ness,

No-bod-y's busi-ness, busi-ness,

No-bod-y's busi-ness what I do.

2. I've got a wife and she's a daisy,

She won't work and I'm too lazy,

It's nobody's business what I do. *Refrain*

ADD A PART

Recorder, bell, and Autoharp players can add other tone colors to a performance of "Nobody's Business."

On the recording of *The Four Seasons*, you will hear string instruments played two ways. Can you tell how they are different?

Vivaldi: *The Four Seasons* (Winter)

HOW GOOD ARE YOUR EARS?

In each of the first five verses in "German Instrument Song," you will hear a different instrument play in the B section. What do you think will happen in verse 6?

German Instrument Song

FOLK SONG FROM GERMANY

ENGLISH WORDS BY TULLA STATLER

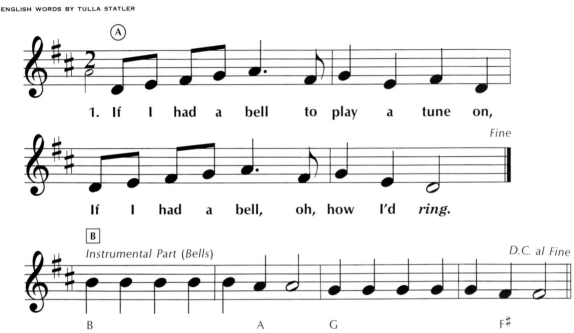

1. If I had a bell to play a tune on,
   If I had a bell, oh, how I'd *ring*.

B Instrumental Part (Bells)

B   A   G   F♯

2. If I had a fiddle, fiddle, fiddle,
   If I had a fiddle, how I'd *bow*.

3. If I had a pipe to play a tune on,
   If I had a pipe, oh, how I'd *blow*.

4. If I had an Autoharp to play on,
   If I had an Autoharp, I'd *strum*.

5. If I had a drum that I could play on,
   If I had a drum, oh, how I'd *beat*.

6. Now we have a tune to play together,
   Now we have a tune, oh, how we'll *play*.

Before you try to play section B on the bells, look at the notes to see how they move.

136

ADD A PART

Add the tone color of other instruments to the bell part in "German Instrument Song."

When the instruments play together, you hear *harmony.*

CALL CHART 7: *Tone Color* 🎵

Some musical sounds are made by voices. Others are made by instruments.

When a number is called, look at the pictures to discover how the sound is made. Match the sounds with the pictures.

1. The *DULCIMER* is strummed, plucked, or struck with mallets.

2. The *BASS DRUM* is struck.

3. To play the *ORGAN,* the player strikes the keys; a machine blows air across and through the pipes.

4. In an electronic laboratory, electric machines make sounds.

5. The player strikes the keys of the *PIANO.* Hammers then strike the strings. Sometimes the player may strike, pluck, or strum the strings without using the keys.

6. The *BASSOON* is played by blowing.

7. The *TIMPANI* are struck with mallets.

8. A *GUITAR* can be strummed or plucked. Sometimes the player strikes the body of the guitar.

Old Bald Eagle
Ibert: "Parade"
Mozart: *Adagio and Fugue in C Minor*
Ussachevsky: *Four Miniatures No. 1*

Satie: "Le Water-Chute"
Nielson: *Quintet Op. 43*
Rooker: *Horn in the West,* "Drum Theme"
McHugh: *Vegetables II*

Forty-Nine Angels

WORDS AND MUSIC BY ROBERT SCHMERTZ

FROM A PICTURE BOOK OF SONGS AND BALLADS BY ROBERT SCHMERTZ. USED BY PERMISSION.

For-ty-nine an-gels look-ing down, Sev-en all a-round a gold-en crown,
For-ty-nine an-gels look-ing down, Sev-en weav-ing lin - en for a gown,

Sev-en with a harp and sev-en with a horn Play for the Ba - by
Sev-en to em-broid-er, sev-en to a-dorn A dress for the Ba - by

new - ly born, Play for the Ba - by new-ly born.
new - ly born, A dress for the Ba - by new-ly born.

And where are the rest of the for-ty - nine? One takes a star, makes it

bright - ly shine; Two tell the news o - ver Gal - i - lee;

Three show the way to the Wise Men three; And lit - tle For - ty - Nine this

bless - ed morn Sings for the Ba - by new - ly born,

Sings for the Ba - by new - ly born.

When each number is called, decide what tone color you hear.

Listen. Then circle your answer.

---

1 TRUMPET AND TROMBONE   FLUTE   CLARINET   AUTOHARP

---

2 TRUMPET AND TROMBONE   FLUTE   CLARINET   AUTOHARP

---

3 TRUMPET AND TROMBONE   FLUTE   CLARINET   AUTOHARP

---

4 TRUMPET AND TROMBONE   FLUTE   CLARINET   AUTOHARP

---

5 TRUMPET AND TROMBONE   FLUTE   CLARINET   AUTOHARP

Debussy: *Syrinx*
Mozart: *Concerto for Clarinet and Orchestra*, K. 622, "Adagio"
Eddleman: *Autoharp Sound Piece*
Gabrieli: *Canzona Noni Toni*
Messiaen: *Abyss of the Birds*

Style: *Old and New*

Music has styles, too.

How many of these things can you hear in this piece?

🎧 Mozart: *Horn Concerto in E♭*

1	*STEADY BEAT*
2	*BEATS MOVING IN TWOS*
3	*LONG AND SHORT PHRASES*
4	*TONAL (FOCUSES ON THE IMPORTANT TONE)*
5	*MELODY WITH HARMONY*
6	*TONE COLOR: FRENCH HORN AND ORCHESTRA*

Listen to another piece.

Do you think it is in the same style, or does it sound different?

🎧 Phillips: *California Dreamin'*

1	*STEADY BEAT*
2	*BEATS MOVING IN TWOS*
3	*LONG AND SHORT PHRASES*
4	*TONAL (FOCUSES ON ONE IMPORTANT TONE)*
5	*MELODY WITH HARMONY*
6	*TONE COLOR: BASS GUITAR, DRUMS, TRUMPETS, ORGAN, VOICES*

Just as cars in different styles can have some of the same parts, pieces of music in different styles can have some of the same parts. The same parts can create a different look or sound, called *style*.

Phrases

FOLLOWING THE PHRASE LINES

Follow along in your book as you listen to this song.
Notice the phrase lines above the music. Are they all
the same length, or are some long and some short?

How D'ye Do and Shake Hands
MUSIC BY OLIVER WALLACE

WORDS BY CY COBEN
© 1951 WALT DISNEY MUSIC COMPANY. REPRINTED BY PERMISSION.

You go through life and nev - er know the day when fate may bring

A sit - u - a - tion that will prove to be em - bar - rass - ing.

Your face gets red, you hide your head, and wish that you could die,____

But that's old - fash - ioned, here's a new thing you should real - ly try.

Sing from here to the end four times.

Say "How d' ye do" and shake hands, Shake hands, shake hands,

Say "How d' ye do" and shake hands, State your name and bus' - ness.

Listen for the long and short phrases in this music.

Hovahness: *Fantasy on Japanese Woodprints*

Poems have phrases, too. After you have listened to the recording, decide how long or short the phrases will be when you read these poems.

PAPER I

Paper is two kinds, to write on, to wrap with.

If you like to write, you write.

If you like to wrap, you wrap.

Some papers like writers, some like wrappers.

Are you a writer or a wrapper?

Carl Sandburg

APRIL FOOL'S DAY

Look out! Look out! You've spilt the ink.

You're sitting in a purple puddle.

Your pants are ripped and I should think

You'd hate to have a nose so pink

And hair in such a dreadful muddle.

Look out! Behind you there's a rat.

He's hiding now behind the stool.

He's going to jump upon your hat.

Look out! Watch out! Oh dear, what's THAT?

It's only you, you April fool!

Marnie Pomeroy

TRACING A RAINBOW

Children in Hawaii use their hands and arms to tell about the rainbow. Follow the phrase lines and trace a rainbow shape in the air for each phrase.

Hawaiian Rainbows

HAWAIIAN FOLK SONG

Ha - wai - ian rain - bows, white clouds roll by;

You show your col - ors a - gainst the sky.

Ha - wai - ian rain - bows, it seems to me,

Reach from the moun - tain down to the sea.

You Can't Make a Turtle Come Out

WORDS AND MUSIC BY MALVINA REYNOLDS   © COPYRIGHT 1962 BY SCHRODER MUSIC CO. (ASCAP) USED BY PERMISSION.

Listen for the longest phrase in this song about a turtle.

1. You can't make a tur - tle come out,

You can't make a tur - tle come out,

You can call him or coax him or shake him or shout,

But you can't make a tur - tle come out, come out,

You can't make a tur - tle come out.

2. If he wants to stay in his shell, (*2 times*)

   You can knock on the door but you can't ring the bell,

   And you can't make a turtle come out, come out,

   You can't make a turtle come out.

3. Be kind to your four-footed friends, (*2 times*)

   A poke makes a turtle retreat at both ends,

   And you can't make a turtle come out, come out,

   You can't make a turtle come out.

4. So you'll have to patiently wait, (*2 times*)

   And when he gets ready he'll open the gate,

   But you can't make a turtle come out, come out,

   You can't make a turtle come out.

5. And when you forget that he's there, (*2 times*)

   He'll be walking around with his head in the air,

   But you can't make a turtle come out, come out,

   You can't make a turtle come out.

STRUM, PLUCK, STRIKE

Make up your own phrase of sound
by following one of the parts below.
Make the phrase as long or as
short as you wish.

On Autoharp

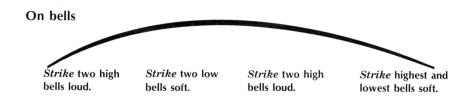

Strum from left
to right.

Pluck a high string
and let it ring.

Pluck a low string
and let it ring.

Stop sound with
your hand or arm.

On bells

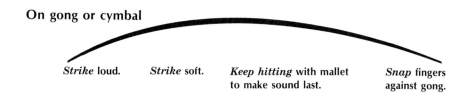

Strike two high
bells loud.

Strike two low
bells soft.

Strike two high
bells loud.

Strike highest and
lowest bells soft.

On gong or cymbal

Strike loud.

Strike soft.

Keep hitting with mallet
to make sound last.

Snap fingers
against gong.

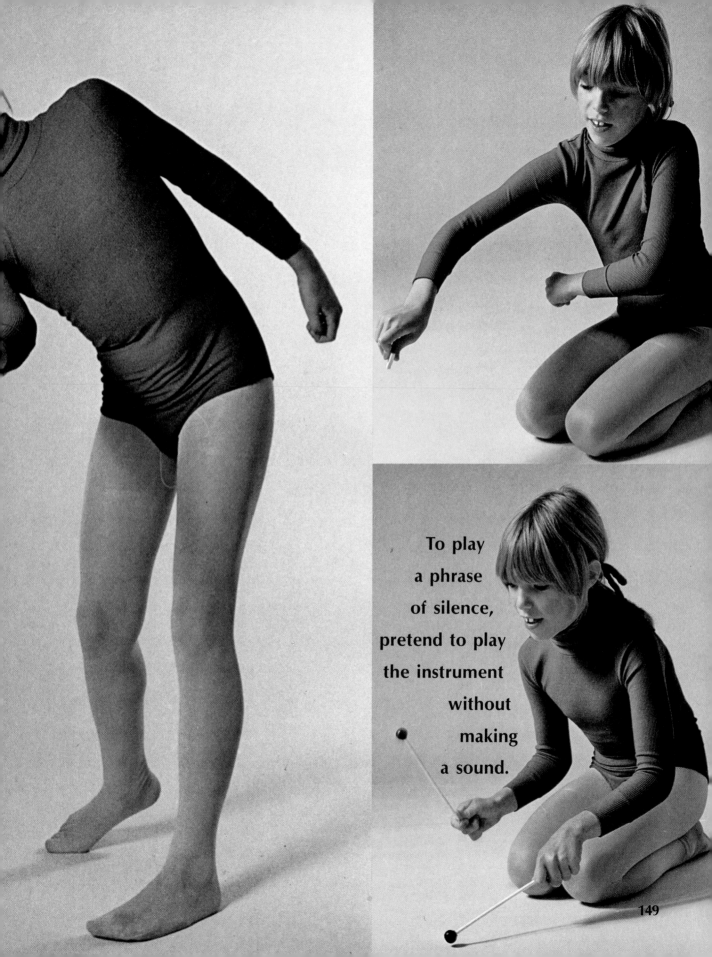

To play
a phrase
of silence,
pretend to play
the instrument
without
making
a sound.

149

SOUND PIECE 4: *Sound and Silent Motion*   ELIZABETH CROOK

Play a phrase of *sound* on the Autoharp, bells, gong,
or cymbal.

Show a phrase of silence by pretending to play.

Now put the phrases together in ABA form.

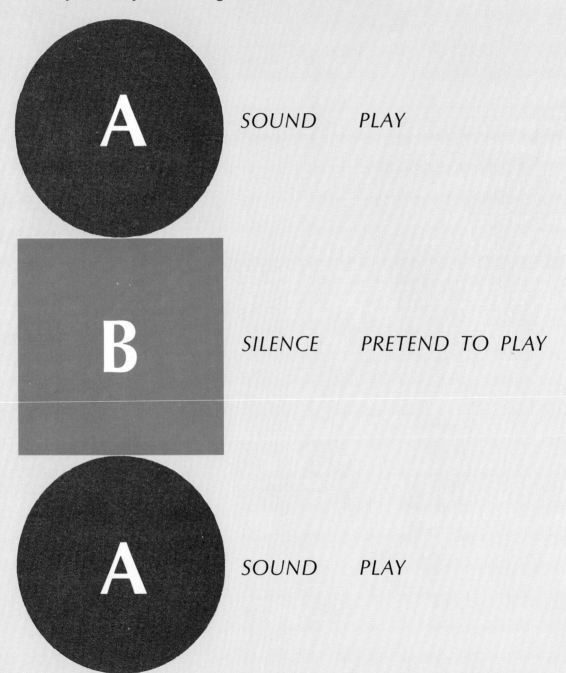

A   *SOUND*   *PLAY*

B   *SILENCE*   *PRETEND TO PLAY*

A   *SOUND*   *PLAY*

CALL CHART 8: *Phrases* 🎵

**Can you feel the length of the phrases in songs
you know?**

Listen for the number of phrases in each song.

Then look at the chart to see if you are right.

---

1. **FOUR**   Oh, What a Beautiful City

---

2. **FOUR**   Join into the Game

---

3. **SIX**   Oh, Susanna

---

4. **TWO**   Hana ichi momme

---

5. **ONE**   The Mad Man

CADENCE: STRONG, WEAK

The ending of a phrase is called a *cadence*. Listen to the recording to hear which phrase ends with a STRONG cadence.

Joyous Chanukah

HEBREW FOLK SONG   ENGLISH WORDS BY PHYLLIS RESNICK

Cha - nu - kah, Cha - nu - kah, hol - i - day so fair,

Glow - ing light, can - dles bright, hap - pi - ness we share.

Gai - ly dance, gai - ly sing while the drey - dl whirls,

Round and round, round and round, see how fast it twirls.

Tambourine

Play
4 times

Shake

Recorder or Bells

SING A DANCE

Listen for the clap at the end of each phrase in this dance song from Israel. How many times do the children clap as they sing the song on the recording?

Debka hora   FOLK SONG FROM ISRAEL

USED BY PERMISSION OF © LAWSON-GOULD MUSIC PUBLISHERS, INC.

When you sing the song, try playing the "claps" on a tambourine.

When you hear the recording again, listen for the strong and weak cadences.

153

Shepherds Bring Candy and Milk

17TH-CENTURY CHRISTMAS SONG FROM BELGIUM   ENGLISH WORDS BY SALLI TERRI
FROM BELGIAN CHRISTMAS SONGS, SET I © 1971 BY LAWSON-GOULD MUSIC PUBLISHERS, INC. USED BY PERMISSION

Listen to the recording and decide how many phrases there are in this song.

Shep-herds, bring can-dy and milk to the Child.

See lit-tle Je-sus cry - ing there.

Hang up your coats to keep out the wind.

Jo-seph is rock-ing the Ba - by so mild.

2. Mary and angels are singing a song,

   There in the stable shabby and bare.

   Joseph so weary comes from the stream.

   He washed the swaddling clothes all the day long.

3. Mary and Jesus are lying there.

   Joseph is gath'ring wood for the fire.

   See how he tends to all of the chores.

   He loves the Baby and Mary fair.

This time, listen for strong and weak cadences. Here is a clue—two are weak and two are strong.

154

WHAT DO YOU HEAR? 10: *Phrases (Cadence)* 🎵
8

Can you hear strong and weak cadences in music?
Decide whether the phrase ends with a strong cadence
or a weak cadence. Listen, then circle your answer.

1	STRONG	WEAK
2	STRONG	WEAK
3	STRONG	WEAK
4	STRONG	WEAK

Join into the Game

1	STRONG	WEAK
2	STRONG	WEAK
3	STRONG	WEAK
4	STRONG	WEAK
5	STRONG	WEAK
6	STRONG	WEAK

Oh, Susanna

The Arts: *Varying a Subject*

Look at the pictures on the opposite page. Each one has the same subject—a very famous man. Do you know his name?

Now, listen to a musical subject, or *theme*. Have you ever heard this little melody before?

Stamitz: *Sonate for Viola d'amore and Viola* (theme)

CALL CHART 9: *Theme and Variations*

Now listen to the same theme played in several different ways.
As each number is called, look at the chart.
It will help you hear many variations of this same subject.

1.	*SUBJECT*	*LOUD, FAST*
2.	*FIRST VARIATION*	*CHANGE OF RHYTHM PATTERNS*
3.	*SECOND VARIATION*	*SOFT, SLOW*
4.	*THIRD VARIATION*	*VERY FAST, MANY SHORT NOTES*

Stamitz: *Sonate for Viola d'amore and Viola*

The Arts: *Focus/No Focus*

On this page you see a picture of five little dolls. The dolls' heads all point to one place—the center. When you look at the dolls your eyes go to the center, too. The center is the focus of interest.

Do your eyes go to one place when you look at the picture of the dolls on page 159?

Look at the paintings on the next two pages. Can you *see* which painting has a center of interest? Some music has focus. Some does not. Can you hear which piece of music has focus?

🎯 Handel: *Water Music,* "Air"

🎯 Ives: *The Cage*

In painting, *focus* refers to a *center of interest* for your eyes to see. In music, *focus* refers to a *sound* for your ears to hear.

Pollock: *Number 27*

Jackson Pollock. NUMBER 27. 1950. Oil on canvas 49 X 106. Collection Whitney Museum of American Art

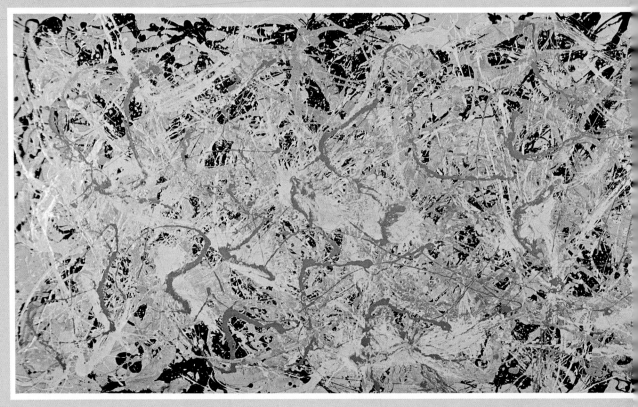

Balla: *Street Light*

BALLA, GIACOMO, STREET LIGHT. LAMPADA-STUDIO DI LUCCI, 1909. OIL ON CANVAS, 68¼ X 45¼.
COLLECTION THE MUSEUM OF MODERN ART, NEW YORK, HILLMAN PERIODICALS FUND.

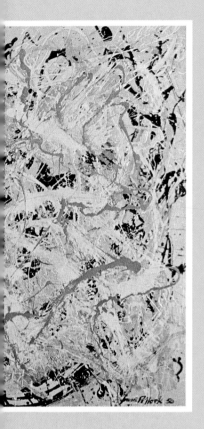

161

Tonality

ONE IMPORTANT TONE

The important tone in this song is G. Play the
G bell on the last word in every verse.

The Mad Man

AMERICAN FOLK TUNE   WORDS BY JEANNE WILHELMS

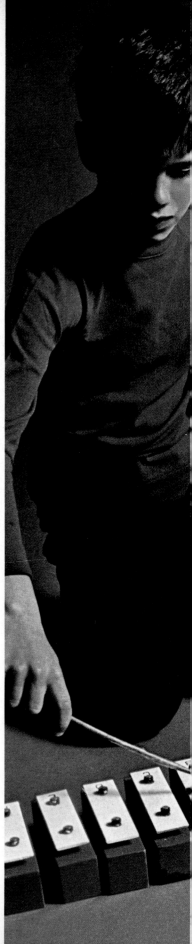

1. In old - en days there was a man

And he fell in a fry - ing pan.

2. The frying pan it was so nice
   And he fell in a bag of ice.

3. The bag of ice it turned to slush
   And he fell in a pan of mush.

4. The pan of mush it was so cold
   And he fell in a pot of gold.

5. The pot of gold it was so rich
   And he fell in a muddy ditch.

6. The muddy ditch it was so deep
   And he fell in a flock of sheep.

7. The flock of sheep did moan and groan
   And he fell in an ice-cream cone.

8. The ice-cream cone it was so sweet
   And he fell on his own two feet.

FOCUS ON G

Here are four bell parts to play with "The Mad Man." Each part *focuses* on the tone G. Part 1 uses low G. Part 2 uses high G. Which G will you play in part 3 and part 4?

You can play one of the bell parts all through the song, or you might want to try a different part for each verse.

TWO DIFFERENT SOUNDS

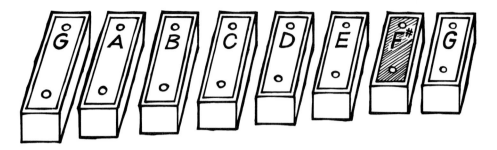

Line up the bells to match the diagram above. When you play these bells upward and downward, you are playing a G *scale.* You feel a pull toward the important tone G.

When music focuses on one important tone, it is called *tonal.* This song is *tonal.* Can you tell why?

Ol' Clo'

TRADITIONAL ROUND

FROM GIRL SCOUT SONG BOOK, P. 91 AS PUBLISHED IN 1925 BY GIRL SCOUTS, INC.

My un - cle he sells ol' clo',

He's a deal - er in chi - na, you know;

And wher - ev - er you go, when you hear "Ol' clo',"

My un - cle is there, you know.

Line up twelve bells to match the diagram above.

When you play these bells upward and downward you are playing a tone row. You feel *no* pull toward an important tone.

When there is no focus on one important tone, the music is called *atonal*. This song is *atonal*. Can you tell why?

Ol' Clo'

MUSIC BY DORIS HAYS

Listen to two pieces for instruments. Which is tonal?

Which is atonal? Schoenberg: *Trio for Violin, Viola, and Cello*   Haydn: *Symphony No. 94*

TONAL OR ATONAL?

Listen to this old familiar song. It is *tonal.* Can you tell why?

Twinkle, Twinkle, Little Star

TRADITIONAL

Twin - kle, twin - kle, lit - tle star, How I won - der what you are,

Up a - bove the world so high, Like a dia - mond in the sky.

Now listen to this "Twinkle, Twinkle, Little Star" song.

It is *atonal.* Can you tell why?

Twinkle, Twinkle, Little Star

MUSIC BY DAVID EDDLEMAN
WORDS TRADITIONAL

Twin - kle, twin - kle, lit - tle star,

How I won - der what you are,

Up a - bove the world so high,

Like a dia - mond in the sky.

WHAT DO YOU HEAR? 11: *Tonality*

Some of the following pieces are *tonal* music.

Other pieces are *atonal* music.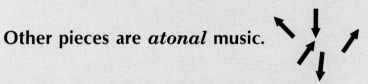

As each number is called, decide whether the music is
tonal, or atonal. Listen. Then circle what you hear.

| 1 | TONAL | ATONAL | Handel: *Water Music,* "Air" |

| 2 | TONAL | ATONAL | Schoenberg: *Trio for Violin, Viola, Cello* |

| 3 | TONAL | ATONAL | Ravosa: *Love* |

| 4 | TONAL | ATONAL | Hays: *Ol' Clo'* |

| 5 | TONAL | ATONAL | Mozart: *Three German Dances,* No. 3 |

| 6 | TONAL | ATONAL | Subotnick: *Touch* |

Rhythm Patterns

TWO SOUNDS TO ONE BEAT

As you listen to the recording of this song, tap the steady beat.

Yesterday Morning

FOLK SONG FROM COLOMBIA

ENGLISH WORDS BY JOAN GILBERT VAN POZNAK

FROM UNICEF BOOK OF CHILDREN'S SONGS, COMPILED AND WITH PHOTOGRAPHS BY WILLIAM I. KAUFMAN, COPYRIGHT 1970 BY WILLIAM I. KAUFMAN, PUBLISHED BY STACKPOLE BOOKS.

1. Oh, yes-ter-day at morn-ing, And then to-day at dawn,

Oh, yes-ter-day at morn-ing, And then to-day at dawn,

The tur-tle-doves were sing-ing, The roost-ers sang a-long,

REFRAIN

Ki-ki-ri, ki-ki-ri, I'm hap-py as can be;

Ki-ki-ri, ki-ki-ri, But who a-wak-en'd me?

2. The dogs for miles and miles
Were barking at the moon, } (2 times)
A silly goose was cackling,
And thought she sang a tune, *Refrain*

3. A heavy rain was falling,
And when it rains it pours, } (2 times)
With thunder, wind and lightning,
I wish I had some oars, *Refrain*

168

ADD A PART

Which instrument will you play to accompany "Yesterday Morning"?

If you choose the drum part, you will play the steady beat. If you choose the maracas part, how many sounds will you play for each of the drum beats?

Drum

Maracas

ADD ANOTHER PART

When you can play the drum part and the maracas part, you might want to try one of these rhythm patterns to play with "Yesterday Morning."

Play the pattern all through the song.

Guiro

Woodblock

THREE SOUNDS TO ONE BEAT

Find the beats divided in three in this song.

Lemons

FOLK SONG FROM PUERTO RICO   ENGLISH WORDS BY ELIZABETH S. BACHMAN

1. A sil - ly old bird in a lem - on tree

Just sat the whole day through;

A sil - ly old bird in a lem - on tree

Just sat the whole day through.

Ah, 'tis true! Ah, 'tis true!

A sil - ly old bird in a lem - on tree

Just sat, and all that he could see

170

Were yel - low lem - ons hang - ing on the tree.

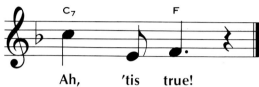

Ah, 'tis true!

2. He grabbed a lemon and took a bite, ⎫
   Then made an awful face. ⎬ (2 times)
   ⎭
   Ah, 'tis true! Ah, 'tis true!

   He bit the lemon and made a face,

   I guess he didn't like the taste

   Of the yellow lemons hanging on the tree. Ah, 'tis true!

3. That silly old bird was very mad, ⎫
   He shook the lemon tree. ⎬ (2 times)
   ⎭
   Ah, 'tis true! Ah, 'tis true!

   That silly old bird was mad, you see,

   With all his might he shook the tree,

   And sent the lemons crashing down on me. Ah, 'tis true!

Take turns playing one of these parts with the recording as others sing.

Guiro

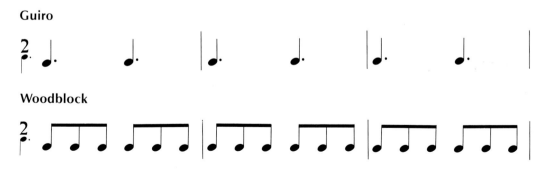

Woodblock

Which instrument plays the beat?

Which instrument plays the beat divided in three?

Find the sign that shows that each measure has two beats.

Find space
in the room
to gallop. Play the
pattern
made by
the sound of
galloping feet.

Find the pattern below.

1.

2.

3.

Now hear all three patterns in
this music. Anonymous:
Dadme Albricias, Hijos d'Eva

173

METER GAMES

Before you begin, choose a percussion instrument and practice playing

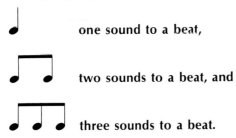

one sound to a beat,

two sounds to a beat, and

three sounds to a beat.

Choose one of the games to play.

To play either game, choose a partner.
You play the boxes in one direction and your partner plays in the other direction at the same time.

The numbers in the boxes
tell you how many sounds to play for each beat.

Follow the arrows and play the boxes,
going first in one direction, then in the other.

When there are two boxes side by side, play either one or the other.

You will need to set a steady beat before you begin!

If both of you make the same choice when you reach the boxes at the end, *you* win a point.
If you choose different boxes, your partner wins a point.
After five games, count up your points.

Another time, try the other game.

Game I

Game II

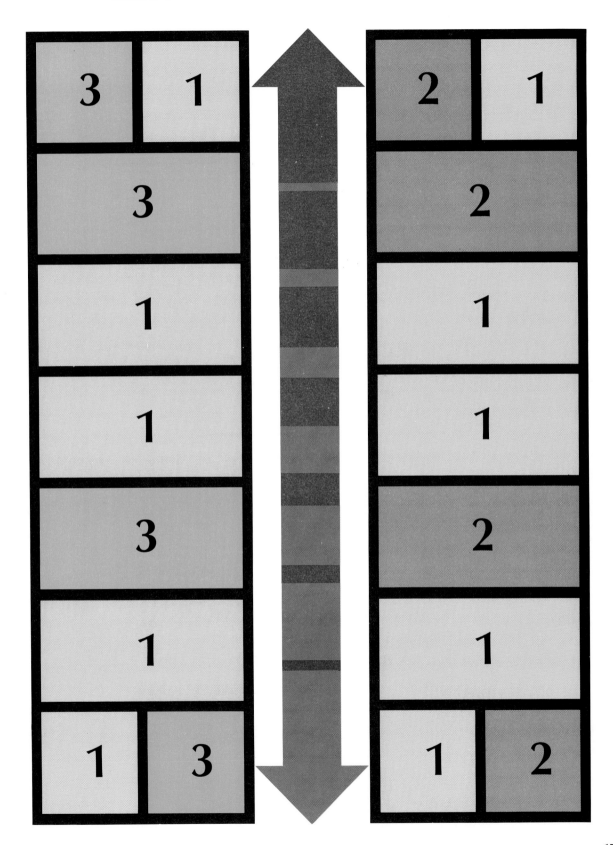

TWO PATTERNS FOR PERCUSSION

Can you guess what a "penny bap and a clipe of ham" means?

The Wee Falorie Man

FOLK SONG FROM IRELAND   COLLECTED BY DAVID HAMMOND

1. I am the wee Fa - lo - rie man,
2. I am a good old work - in' man,

A rat - tlin', rov - in' I - rish - man,
Each day I carry my wee tin can,

1. I can do all that ev - er you can,
2. A large pen - ny bap and a clipe of ham,

For I am the wee Fa - lo - rie man.
7. I am a good old work - in' man.

3. I am the wee Falorie man,   I can do all that ever you can,
   A rattlin', rovin' Irishman,   For I am the wee Falorie man.

Here are two rhythm patterns to play all through the song. Which one will you choose?

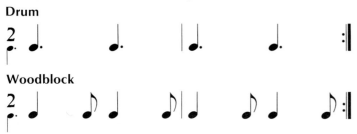

Drum

Woodblock

176

The Old Man

FOLK SONG FROM CANADA

FROM TRADITIONAL SONGS FROM NOVA SCOTIA BY HELEN CREIGHTON. REPRINTED BY PERMISSION OF McGRAW-HILL RYERSON LIMITED.

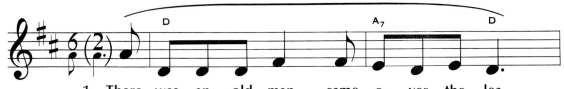

1. There was an old man came o-ver the lea,
2. My moth-er she bade me o-pen the door,

Ho, ho, ho, but I won't have him!
Ho, ho, ho, but I won't have him!

He came o-ver the lea I sup-pose to see me
I____ o-pened the door and he bowed to the floor

With his long beard so new - ly shav-en.
With his long beard so new - ly shav-en.

3. My mother she bade me set him a chair,

   Ho, ho, ho, but I won't have him!

   I set him a chair, but I didn't care

   For his long beard so newly shaven.

4. My mother, she bade me give him some meat,

   Ho, ho, ho, but I won't have him!

   I gave him some meat, but he wouldn't eat

   With his long beard so newly shaven.

5. My mother she bade me sit on his knee,

   Ho, ho, ho, but I won't have him!

   For I sat on his knee and he tried to kiss me

   With his long beard so newly shaven.

177

Style: Modern

New things create a *modern style* of living.
New sounds create *modern styles* of music.

Follow the pictures as you listen to examples in modern styles.

🎵 *Modern Sounds*

Hardin (arr.): *Lonesome Valley*

Arel: *Stereo Electronic Music No. 1*

Erb: *Phantasama*

Oliveros: *Sound Patterns*

Modern music has many different styles for you to enjoy.

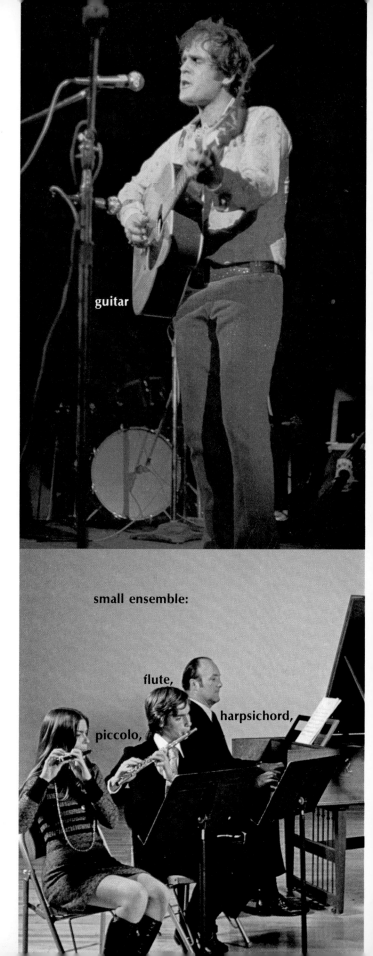

guitar

small ensemble:

flute,

piccolo,

harpsichord,

voice sounds

string bass

English horn,

oboe

electronic
studio

Intervals: *Steps, Leaps, Repeats*

Do the tones in the chorus parts step, leap, or repeat?

Hill an' Gully

CALYPSO FROM JAMAICA   ENGLISH WORDS BY MARGARET MARKS

REFRAIN

Hill an' gul - ly rid - er, Hill an'___ gul - ly.

Hill an' gul - ly rid - er, Hill an'___ gul - ly.

VERSE

1. Took my horse an' come down, Hill an'___ gul - ly.

But my horse done stum - ble down, Hill an'___ gul - ly.

An' the night-time come an' tum - ble down, Hill an'___ gul - ly.

2. Oh, the moon shine bright down,

   Hill an' gully.

   Ain't no place to hide in down,

   Hill an' gully.

   An' a zombie come a-ridin' down,

   Hill an' gully.

3. Oh, my knees they shake down,

   Hill an' gully.

   An' my heart starts quakin' down,

   Hill an' gully.

   Ain't nobody goin' to get me down,

   Hill an' gully.

4. That's the last I set down,

   Hill an' gully.

   Pray the Lord don' let me down,

   Hill an' gully.

   An' I run till daylight breakin' down,

   Hill an' gully.

Old House

AMERICAN FOLK GAME SONG   COLLECTED BY JOHN W. WORK

Sing the chorus parts. Which ones use only repeated tones?

Which ones use a leap?

1. Old house. Tear it down!
   Who's going to help me? Tear it down!
   Bring me a hammer. Tear it down!
   Bring me a saw. Tear it down!
   Next thing you bring me, Tear it down!
   Is a wrecking machine. Tear it down!

2. New house. Build it up!
   Who's going to help me? Build it up!
   Bring me a hammer. Build it up!
   Bring me a saw. Build it up!
   Next thing you bring me, Build it up!
   Is a carpenter man. Build it up!

INTERVAL CHECKUP

How does the melody work?

Do the tones repeat, move by step, or leap?

Play these melodies on bells or recorder.

1.

2.

3.

4.

5.

America

TRADITIONAL   WORDS BY SAMUEL FRANCIS SMITH

Does this melody move mostly by *steps*, or by *leaps*?

To find out, follow the notes as you sing the song.

My coun-try! 'tis   of thee, Sweet land of lib - er - ty,

Of thee I   sing;   Land where my fa - thers died,

Land of the Pil - grims' pride, From ev - 'ry___ moun - tain - side

Let___ free - dom   ring!

My native country, thee, Land of the noble free,

Thy name I love; I love thy rocks and rills,

Thy woods and templed hills, My heart with rapture thrills

Like that above.

Our fathers' God, to Thee, Author of liberty,

To Thee we sing; Long may our land be bright

With freedom's holy light; Protect us by Thy might,

Great God, our King!

Does the instrumental part move mostly by *steps*, or by *leaps*?

A LEAP FROM
HIGH
TO
LOW

This patriotic song has steps, leaps, and repeats.

Listen for the two words "America, America" as you sing. On which one does the melody leap from low to high?

America, the Beautiful MUSIC BY SAMUEL A. WARD   WORDS BY KATHARINE LEE BATES

O beau - ti - ful for spa - cious skies, For am - ber waves of grain,

For pur - ple moun - tain maj - es - ties A - bove the fruit - ed plain!

A - mer - i - ca! A - mer - i - ca! God shed His grace on thee

And crown thy good with broth - er - hood From sea to shin - ing sea!

Recorder or bells

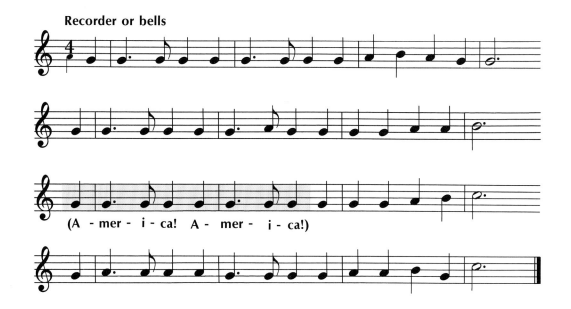

(A - mer - i - ca! A - mer - i - ca!)

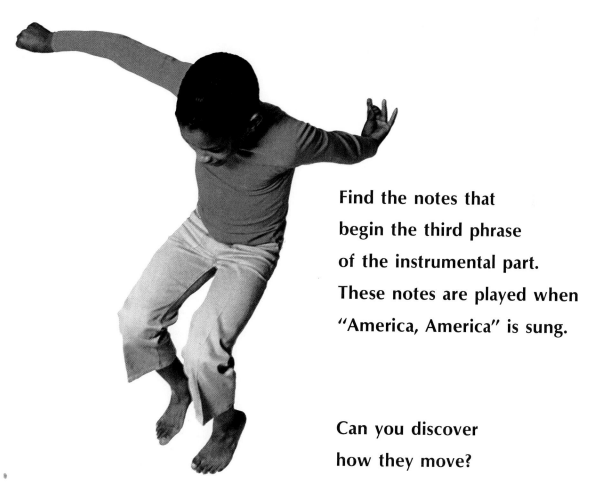

Find the notes that
begin the third phrase
of the instrumental part.
These notes are played when
"America, America" is sung.

Can you discover
how they move?

A SONG WITH FOUR ENDINGS

This song is fun to sing. Follow the notes as you listen
to the recording. This will help you learn to sing it.
Look for notes that repeat, move by step, or by leap.

Wonders Never Cease

YIDDISH FOLK SONG

ENGLISH WORDS BY ELIZABETH S. BACHMAN
"HOB ICH A POR OKSN" FROM A TREASURY OF JEWISH FOLKSONG EDITED BY RUTH RUBIN. COPYRIGHT ©1950 BY SCHOCKEN BOOKS INC. REPRINTED BY PERMISSION OF SCHOCKEN BOOKS INC.

1. I've a pair of ox - en, ox - en,

Ox - en who cut noo - dles, noo - dles.

Repeat these two measures for additional lines in verses 2–6.

Do you mean you've nev - er seen An ox cut noo - dles by the oo - dles?

Won - ders nev - er cease, Oh, won - ders nev - er cease.

2. I've a pair of bears, bears,

   Bears who sweep the rooms, rooms.

   Do you mean you've never seen

   A bear sweep rooms without a broom?

   An ox cut noodles by the oodles?

   Wonders never cease,

   Oh, wonders never cease.

3. I've a pair of goats, goats,

   Goats who wheel the children, children.

   Do you mean you've never seen

   A goat so glad to wheel a lad?

   A bear sweep rooms without a broom?

   An ox cut noodles by the oodles?

   Wonders . . .

4. I've a pair of dogs, dogs,

Dogs who write with ink, ink.

Do you mean you've never seen

A dog who'd think to write with ink?

A goat so glad to wheel a lad?

A bear sweep rooms without a broom?

An ox cut noodles by the oodles?

Wonders . . .

5. I've a pair of hens, hens,

Hens who gather wood, wood.

Do you mean you've never seen

A hen so good at gath'ring wood?

A dog who'd think to write with ink?

A goat so glad to wheel a lad?

A bear sweep rooms without a broom?

An ox cut noodles by the oodles?

Wonders . . .

6. I've a pair of birds, birds,

Birds who like to bake, bake.

Do you mean you've never seen

A bird who baked a layer cake?

A hen so good at gath'ring wood?

A dog who'd think to write with ink?

A goat so glad to wheel a lad?

A bear sweep rooms without a broom?

An ox cut noodles by the oodles?

Wonders . . .

If you followed the notes as you listened to "Wonders Never Cease," you noticed that the ending, or cadence, looks like this.

Here are three other cadences you can sing at the end of the song. Before you choose one, figure out how the tones move.

1.

3.

2.

THE SHAPE OF A MELODY

Follow the notes as you listen to this song. You will discover that the melody moves upward and downward by steps.

The way tones move gives a melody its shape. Another word for *shape* is "contour."

The Cage
CHARLES E. IVES

A leop - ard went a - round his cage from one side

back to the oth - er side; he stopped_ on - ly when the keep - er

came a - round with meat; A boy who had been there three

hours be - gan to won - der,_____ "Is_____ life an - y - thing

like that?"

As you listen again, draw the contour of the melody in the air with your hand.

Kookaburra

WORDS AND MUSIC BY MARION SINCLAIR

FROM THE DITTY BAG BY JANET E. TOBITT. COPYRIGHT © 1946 BY JANET E. TOBITT. USED BY PERMISSION.

Koo - ka - bur - ra sits on the old gum tree,____

Mer - ry, mer - ry king of the bush is he;____

Laugh, Koo-ka-bur-ra, laugh, Koo-ka-bur-ra, Gay your life must be.

Bells or Recorder

1.

2.

Bells

3.

CALL CHART 10: *Contour*

1.	*STEPWISE*
2.	*LEAPWISE*
3.	*STEPWISE*
4.	*LEAPWISE*

Tchaikovsky: *Symphony No. 6,* Movement 1
Webern: *Five Pieces for Orchestra*
The Wongga
Debussy: "Golliwog's Cakewalk"

FOLLOW THE CONTOUR

Here are parts of songs you may know. Look at the music to see when the notes repeat and when they move upward or downward by step or by leap. Then try playing the parts on the bells.

1.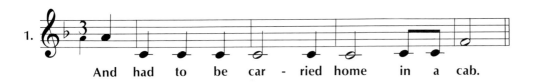

And had to be car - ried home in a cab.

2.

Sab-bath, for a spe - cial treat, there's a 'ta - ter pud - ding!

3.

Would - n't it be chill - y with no skin on!

4. All

Boil them cab-bage down, down.

5.

Ah, 'tis true! Ah, 'tis true!

6.

All the pret - ty lit - tle hors - es.

CALL CHART 11: *Intervals* 🎵

Listen to these melodies as you follow the notes.

Do the tones move mostly by step, mostly by leap,

or mostly by repeated tones?

As you hear each number called, look at the chart

to help you.

1. *LEAPS*

Saint-Saëns: "Kangaroos"

2. *LEAPS*

Bugle Call: *Taps*

3. *REPEATED TONES*

McHugh: *Rain Song*

4. *STEPS*

Handel: *Messiah*, "Pastoral Symphony"

5. *STEPS*

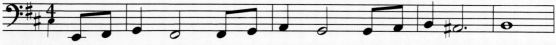

Tchaikovsky: *Symphony No. 6*, Movement 1

1.

2.

3.

There are many ways
to get an idea for the
contour of a melody.

One way is
to look at the
contour of a picture.

How does
the picture in
Column 1 change
in Columns 2 and 3?

SOUND PIECE 5: *Picture Piece*   DAVID S. WALKER

Here are some contour lines taken from the ideas
in the kitten pictures.

Play the tones they suggest to you, on bells or on a
piano.

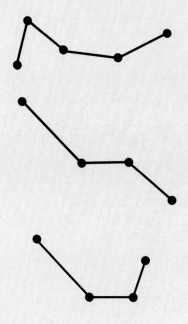

Will you use a steady beat, or no beat?

Will your piece be fast, or slow?

Will you use short sounds, long sounds, or both?

Will your piece move in twos, or threes?

Will it be loud, soft, or will the dynamics change?

Make up your own sound piece, using some of these
ideas.

A LEAP FROM LOW TO HIGH

Look at the contour made by the notes in the color box.

Where do the notes move by step? Find a place where

a note repeats. Look for a leap from low to high.

My Twenty Pennies

FOLK SONG FROM VENEZUELA   TRANSLATION BY J. OLCUTT SANDERS

1. With twen-ty pen-nies, with twen-ty pen-nies,

With twen-ty pen-nies I bought a *pa - va.*

The *pa - va* had a *pa - vi - to,*

Repeat for additional lines in verses 2-6.

I have the *pa - va* and the *pa - vi - to;*

And so I still have my twen-ty pen-nies.

2. With twenty pennies, with twenty pennies,

With twenty pennies I bought a *gata.*

The *gata* had a *gatito,*

I have the *gata* and the *gatito;*

I have the *pava* and the *pavito;*

And so I still have my twenty pennies.

3. . . . *chiva* . . . *chivito* . . .

4. . . . *mona* . . . *monito* . . .

5. . . . *lora* . . . *lorito* . . .

6. . . . *vaca* . . . *vaquito* . . .

194

WHAT DO YOU HEAR? 12: *Intervals* 🔘

Listen to the following pieces. Each time a number is called, decide whether the contour of the melody is mostly stepwise, or mostly leapwise.

Listen. Then circle your answer.

1　*MOSTLY STEPWISE　　MOSTLY LEAPWISE*

Saint-Saëns: *Carnival of the Animals,* "Kangaroos"

2　*MOSTLY STEPWISE　　MOSTLY LEAPWISE*

Ives: *The Cage*

3　*MOSTLY STEPWISE　　MOSTLY LEAPWISE*

For Thy Gracious Blessing

4　*MOSTLY STEPWISE　　MOSTLY LEAPWISE*

Webern: *Five Pieces for Orchestra,* Op. 10, No. 5

5　*MOSTLY STEPWISE　　MOSTLY LEAPWISE*

Bock-Harnick: *Sunrise, Sunset*

6　*MOSTLY STEPWISE　　MOSTLY LEAPWISE*

Debussy: Children's Corner Suite, "Golliwog's Cakewalk"

The Arts: Contour

Which of these lines shows the contour of the phrase endings of "All the Pretty Little Horses?"

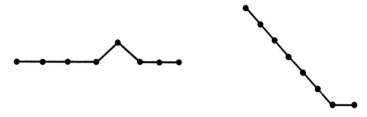

Which of these lines shows the contour of the things you see in the pictures?

1.

2.

FIRE HELMET (WITH EAGLE); INDEX OF AMERICAN DESIGN. NATIONAL GALLERY OF ART, WASHINGTON, D.C.   BARBER POLE; INDEX OF AMERICAN DESIGN. NATIONAL GALLERY OF ART, WASHINGTON, D.C.

SOUND PIECE 6: *Sound Contours*

JOYCE BOGUSKY REIMER

These lines suggest the contour of a melody.
Sing or play a melody of your own that follows
the lines.

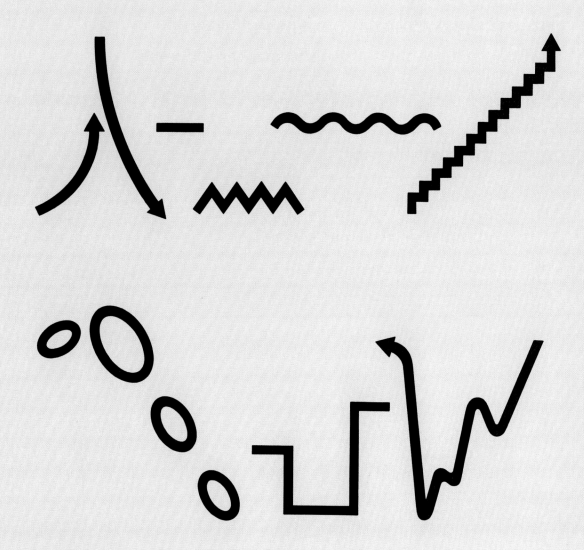

Make up your own sound piece using some of
these ideas.

Texture

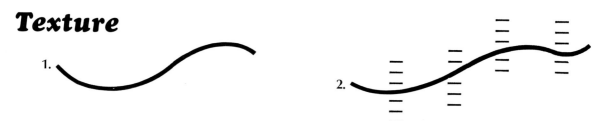

1.

2.

You will hear two performances of this song. As you listen, look at the two diagrams. One diagram shows what is happening in the first performance. The other diagram shows what is happening in the second performance. How are the performances different?

He's Got the Whole World in His Hands

BLACK SPIRITUAL

1. He's got the whole world___ in his hands,___
2. He's got the wind and rain___ in his hands,___
3. He's got both you and me___ in his hands,___

He's got the whole world___ in his hands,___
He's got the wind and rain___ in his hands,___
He's got both you and me___ in his hands,___

He's got the whole world___ in his hands,___
He's got the wind and rain___ in his hands,___
He's got both you and me___ in his hands,___

He's got the whole world in his hands.___
He's got the whole world in his hands.___
He's got the whole world in his hands.___

198

CHANGING THE TEXTURE

Sing this song as a melody alone. Then add harmony by playing the Autoharp chords.

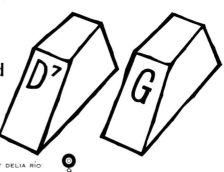

San Sereni

FOLK SONG FROM LATIN AMERICA   ENGLISH WORDS BY DELIA RÍO

1.
2. San Se - re - ni,   I'm a bus - y pa - na - de - ro,
3.

za - pa - te - ro,
car - pin - te - ro,

Work - ing like this   to bake some good pan - ci - tos,
make some good za - pa - tos,
build some good ca - si - tas,

A - work - ing just like this,   a - work - ing just like that.

Here is a harmony part for "San Sereni." What can you discover about the contour of the instrumental part?

Instruments

AN "ADD ON" SONG

Try not to get lost in this "add on" song. Follow the words as you listen to the recording.

When I First Came to This Land

WORDS AND MUSIC BY OSCAR BRAND

1. When I first came to this land, I was not a wealth-y man.

Then I built my-self a shack, I did what I could. I

Repeat these four measures for additional lines in verses 2-5.

called my shack, *Break-my-back.* But the land was sweet and good;

I did what I could.

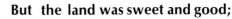

2. When I first came to this land,

   I was not a wealthy man.

   Then I bought myself a cow,

   I did what I could.

   I called my cow, *No-milk-now,*

   I called my shack, *Break-my-back.*

   But the land was sweet and good;

   I did what I could.

3. When I first came to this land,

   I was not a wealthy man.

   Then I bought myself a duck,

   I did what I could.

   I called my duck, *Out-of-luck,*

   I called my cow, *No-milk-now,*

   I called my shack, *Break-my-back.*

   But the land . . .

4. When I first came to this land,

   I was not a wealthy man.

   Then I got myself a wife,

   I did what I could.

   I called my wife, *Run-for-your-life,*

   I called my duck, *Out-of-luck,*

   I called my cow, *No-milk-now,*

   I called my shack, *Break-my-back.*

   But the land . . .

5. When I first came to this land,

   I was not a wealthy man.

   Then I got myself a son,

   I did what I could.

   I called my son, *My-work's-done,*

   I called my wife, *Run-for-your-life,*

   I called my duck, *Out-of-luck,*

   I called my cow, *No-milk-now,*

   I called my shack, *Break-my-back.*

   But the land . . .

ADD A HARMONY PART

Look at the contour made by the notes in the color box. How do the notes move in the ending, or cadence, of the song?

Here are three other cadences you can sing at the end of the song. Before you choose one, figure out how the tones move.

When two endings are sung at the same time, you hear harmony. How else can you add harmony to this song?

This Land Is Your Land

WORDS AND MUSIC BY WOODY GUTHRIE

Woody Guthrie was a folk singer who made up hundreds of songs about the country he loved. What are some of the things he sings about our land in this song?

If you made up a song about your land, what are some of the things you might sing about?

REFRAIN

This land is your land,____ This land is my land____

From Cal - i - for - nia____ to the New York is - land;____

From the red-wood for - est ____ to the Gulf Stream wa - ters;____

Fine

This land was made for you and me.____

VERSE

1. As I was walk - ing____ that rib-bon of high - way,____

I saw a - bove me____ that end - less sky - way.____

202

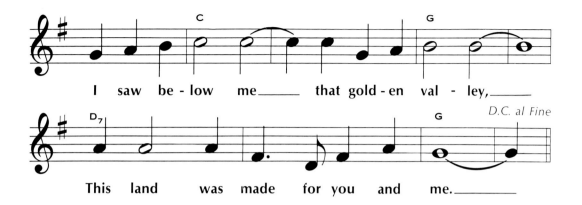

I saw be - low me _____ that gold - en val - ley, _____

D.C. al Fine

This land was made for you and me. _____

2. I've roamed and rambled and I followed my footsteps
   To the sparkling sands of her diamond deserts,
   And all around me a voice was sounding,
   "This land was made for you and me."

3. When the sun comes shining and I was strolling
   And the wheatfields waving and the dust clouds rolling,
   As the fog was lifting a voice was chanting,
   "This land was made for you and me."

To add harmony to "This Land Is Your land,"

· **Play an Autoharp accompaniment.**

· **Play a countermelody on recorder or bells.**

Recorder or Bells

ADD A HARMONY PART

On these two pages you will find bell parts for twelve songs in your book. Choose your favorite song and practice the bell part. When you are ready, play it over and over while others sing the song.

The Tree in the Wood, page 10

Roll an' Rock, page 12

Michie Banjo, page 20

Michie Banjo, page 20

Hey Ho, Hey Lo, page 42

Skin and Bones, page 52

Chicka Hanka, page 54

New Year's Song, page 60

Little David, Play on Your Harp, page 88

Shepherds Came to Bethlehem, page 120

Forty-Nine Angels, page 140

Hill an' Gully, page 180

CHECK THE TEXTURE

You will hear "A Ram Sam Sam" played three ways. As you listen to each performance, look at the diagrams on page 32 in your book and point to the one that shows the texture you are hearing.

A Ram Sam Sam

FOLK SONG FROM MOROCCO

Listen to "A Ram Sam Sam" sung as a round. Follow the music as you listen. Will you follow the part for Voice 1, or the part for Voice 2?

TEXTURE: THICK AND THIN

When you sing "America, the Beautiful" as a melody alone, the texture is *thin.* What happens to the texture when other parts are added to the melody? To find out,

· Sing the melody.

· Add the recorder countermelody (page 185) to the singing.

· Add the accompaniment on the recording to the playing and singing.

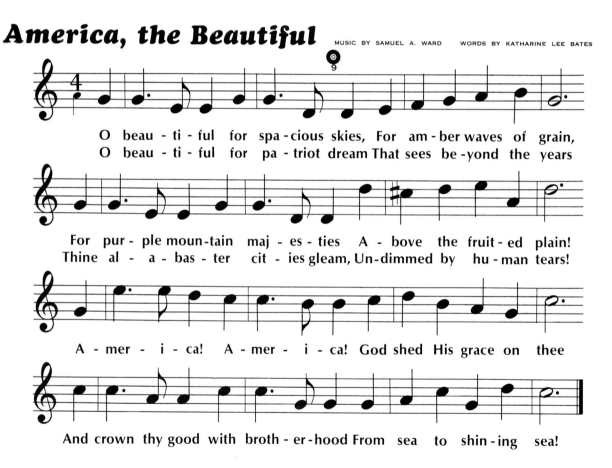

America, the Beautiful

MUSIC BY SAMUEL A. WARD   WORDS BY KATHARINE LEE BATES

O beau - ti - ful for spa - cious skies, For am - ber waves of grain,
O beau - ti - ful for pa - triot dream That sees be -yond the years

For pur - ple moun-tain maj - es - ties A - bove the fruit - ed plain!
Thine al - a - bas - ter cit - ies gleam, Un-dimmed by hu - man tears!

A - mer - i - ca! A - mer - i - ca! God shed His grace on thee

And crown thy good with broth - er -hood From sea to shin - ing sea!

Listen to another version of "America, the Beautiful" on this recording. Is the texture thick, or thin?

Ward: *America, the Beautiful*

CALL CHART 12: *Texture* 🔟

Listen to the recording to discover the *texture* in these songs.

The chart will help you by showing a drawing of the texture you hear.

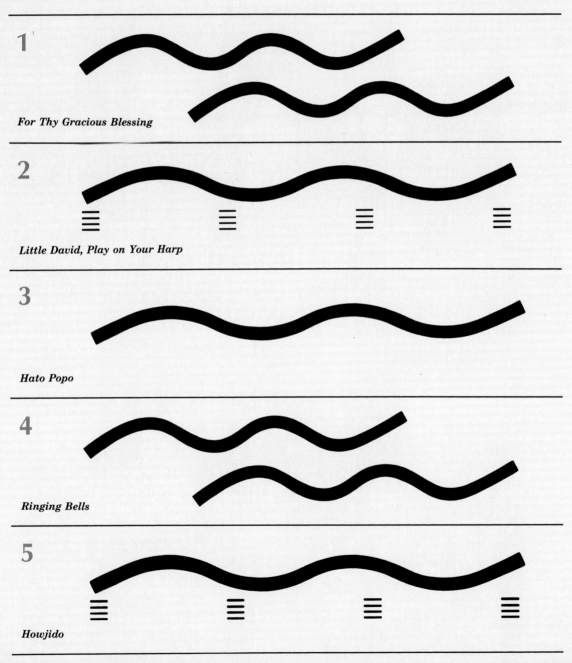

1

For Thy Gracious Blessing

2

Little David, Play on Your Harp

3

Hato Popo

4

Ringing Bells

5

Howjido

WHAT DO YOU HEAR? 13: *Texture* 🔘

When each number is called, decide whether you hear *harmony*, or *no harmony*. Then decide what *tone colors* you hear. Do you hear voices, or instruments, or voices and instruments?

Listen. Then circle everything you hear.

---

1   HARMONY   NO HARMONY

        VOICES   INSTRUMENTS

            VOICES AND INSTRUMENTS

---

2   HARMONY   NO HARMONY

        VOICES   INSTRUMENTS

            VOICES AND INSTRUMENTS

---

3   HARMONY   NO HARMONY

        VOICES   INSTRUMENTS

            VOICES AND INSTRUMENTS

---

4   HARMONY   NO HARMONY

        VOICES   INSTRUMENTS

            VOICES AND INSTRUMENTS

---

5   HARMONY   NO HARMONY

        VOICES   INSTRUMENTS

            VOICES AND INSTRUMENTS

---

6   HARMONY   NO HARMONY

        VOICES   INSTRUMENTS

            VOICES AND INSTRUMENTS

Zynczak: *Love You*

PLAN YOUR OWN TEXTURE

You can sing each of the next two songs as a melody alone. Or you can change the texture of each song by playing an added part.

Listen to the recording of each song. Then decide which song you would like to work on.

El Nacimiento

FOLK SONG FROM PUERTO RICO

San Jo-sé y Ma-rí - a___ a Be-lén lle-ga-ron,___

Pi-die-ron po-sa-da___ y se la ne-ga-ron.___

Sing the melody alone.

Add harmony by playing Autoharp chords.

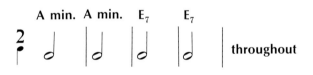

A min. A min. E₇ E₇ | throughout

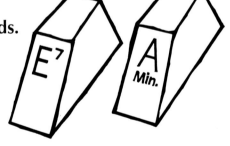

Add a countermelody.

Recorder or Bells

El rorro

CHRISTMAS SONG FROM MEXICO   ENGLISH WORDS BY VERNE MUNOZ

A la ru - ru - ru, ni - ño chi - qui - to,

Fine

Duer - ma - se ya,____ mi Je - su - si - to.____

1. *Now all the an - i - mals their si - lence keep,*____

D.C. al Fine

So they will not dis - turb the In - fant's sleep.

2. *The choirs of holy angels from on high,*
   Foretold the coming of this blessed child.

3. *Oh, night of happiness, oh, night of joy,*
   Guard well the Mother and Her Little Boy.

Ⓐ **Recorder or Bells**

Fine

Ⓑ **Recorder, Violin, Bells**

D.C. al Fine

Play the finger cymbals on the first beat of every measure in section A.

CHANGE THE TEXTURE

Sing this song as a melody alone. The texture will
change when the song is sung as a round.

Melchior and Balthazar

FOLK SONG FROM FRANCE   ENGLISH WORDS BY EMILY VIDAL

1. Mel - chi - or   and Bal - tha - zar

Went up - on   a   jour - ney, Went up - on   a   jour - ney;

Mel - chi - or   and Bal - tha - zar

Went up - on   a   jour - ney far with King Gas - par.

2. When they came to Bethlehem
   They opened up the baskets,
   Opened up the baskets;
   When they came to Bethlehem
   They opened up the baskets
   They had brought with them.

3. Then they ate some cabbage soup.
   They were very hungry,
   Oh, so very hungry;
   Then they ate some cabbage soup.
   They were just as hungry
   As they could be.

Add this bell part all through the song.

Bells

WHAT DO YOU HEAR? 14: *Style* 🔘
10

Each time a number is called, there will be two pieces
played.

Sometimes the two pieces will come from the same
musical family, or style.

Other times the two pieces will be from two different
musical families, or styles.

If you think the two pieces are in the same style, draw
a circle around the word SAME.

If you think the two pieces are in different styles, draw
a circle around the word DIFFERENT.

Listen. Then circle what you hear.

1	*SAME*	*DIFFERENT*	*Idiophone Solo* Ravosa: *Love*
2	*SAME*	*DIFFERENT*	*Buying Fish* *'Taters*
3	*SAME*	*DIFFERENT*	Bach: *Suite No. 3 in D Minor,* "Overture" Bach: *Suite No. 2 in B Minor,* "Overture"
4	*SAME*	*DIFFERENT*	Debussy: *Children's Corner Suite,* "Golliwog's Cakewalk" Ussachevsky: *Four Miniatures,* No. 1
5	*SAME*	*DIFFERENT*	Mozart: *Three German Dances,* No. 3 Mozart: *Horn Concerto in E♭ Major*
6	*SAME*	*DIFFERENT*	Ussachevsky: *Four Miniatures,* No. 1 Hays: *Sound Piece No. 3*
7	*SAME*	*DIFFERENT*	Vivaldi: *The Four Seasons* (winter) Bartók: *Roumanian Dance No. 6*

Style: *Time Lines*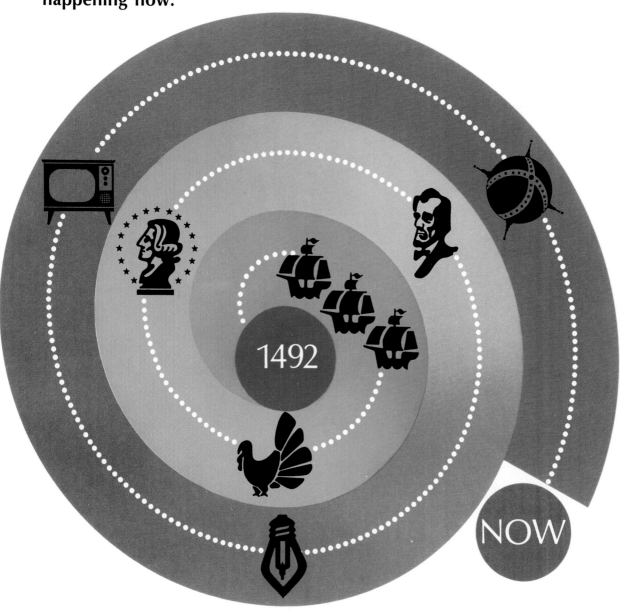

To follow the time line below, put your finger on 1492. Move along the dotted line to find things that happened very long ago right up to things that are happening now.

As you listen to the recording, follow the dotted line in this time line. You will hear music in different styles that was composed at different times. Discover which instruments were used to help create different styles of music.

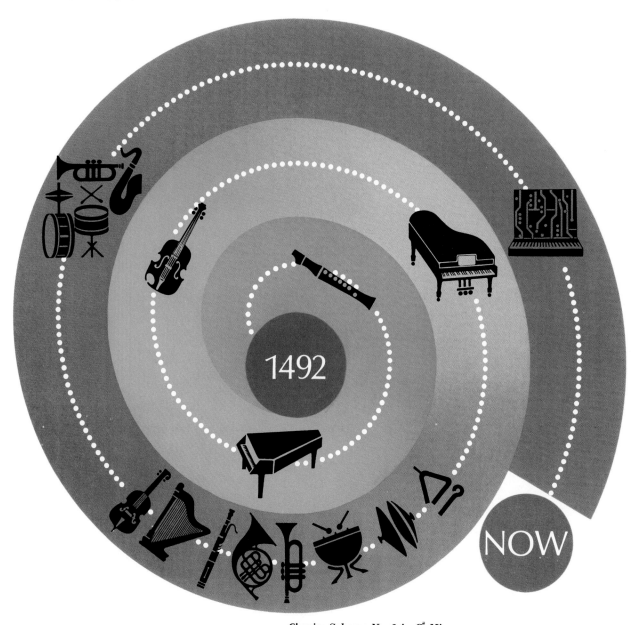

Chopin: *Scherzo No. 3 in C♯ Minor*

Anonymous: *Dadme Albricias, Hijos d'Eva*

Tchaikovsky: *Nutcracker Suite, "Trepak"*

Bach: *Passacaglia in C minor*

Baldridge: *Let's Dance*

Mozart: *Three German Dances*, No. 3

Ussachevsky: *Four Miniatures*, No. 1

Singing about Our Land

Sandy Land

FOLK SONG FROM OKLAHOMA

FROM THE AMERICAN PLAY PARTY SONG BY B. A. BOTKIN
REPRINTED BY PERMISSION OF CURTIS BROWN, LTD. COPYRIGHT © 1937, 1963, BY B. A. BOTKIN

In this folk song from Oklahoma, people sing about making
a living from the land.

What else can you do in sandy land?
Can you think of new verses?

1. Make my liv - in' in sand - y land,

Make my liv - in' in sand - y land,

Make my liv - in' in sand - y land,

La - dies, fare you well.

2. Raise sweet potatoes in sandy land, . . .
   Ladies, fare you well.

3. Dig sweet potatoes in sandy land, . . .
   Ladies, fare you well.

Add an Autoharp part. What chords will you use?

The Crawdad Hole

AMERICAN FOLK SONG

Some people make their living by fishing.

1. Now, you get a line and I'll get a pole,___ Hon - ey,___
2. Oh, sittin' on the bank 'til my feet got___ cold,___ Hon - ey,___

You get a line and I'll get a pole, Babe;_____
Sittin' on the bank 'til my feet got___ cold, Babe,_____

You get a line and I'll get a pole,
Sittin' on the bank 'til my feet got___ cold,

We'll go fish - in' in the craw - dad hole,___ Hon - ey,
Look - in' down___ that___ craw - dad hole,___

Ba - - by mine.___

3. Well, what you gonna do when the pond goes dry, Honey?
   Sit on the bank and catch an old horsefly!

4. Oh, yonder comes a man with a sack on his back, Honey,
   Got more crawdads than he can pack,

5. That man fell down and broke that sack, Honey,
   Watch those crawdads backin' back,

6. Well, sell my crawdads three for a dime, Honey,
   Ain't no crawdads as good as mine,

The Goat

AMERICAN FOLK SONG

Have you ever heard a "tall tale"? Here is one about a
man and his goat.

1. There was   a man, (there was a man), now please take note, (now please, etc.),
2. One day   that goat_____ felt frisk and fine,_____
3. But when   the train_____ hove in - to sight_____

There was   a man_____ who had   a goat._____
Ate   three red shirts_____ from off   the line._____
That   goat grew pale_____ and green with fright._____

He loved that goat,_____ in - deed he did,_____
The man,   he grabbed_____ him   by   the back_____
He heaved a   sigh_____ as   if   in pain,_____

He   loved that   goat_____ just like   a kid._____
And   tied him   to_____ a   rail - road track._____
Coughed up those shirts_____ and flagged the train._____

Play a long bell sound on the notes in the color boxes.

You will need these notes.

G   A   B   C

Oleana

NORWEGIAN EMIGRANT SONG   ENGLISH WORDS BY POLLY BUDD   11

The people who came to our country settled in many
different places. Some farmers from Norway thought
Oleana would be a good place to be.

1. O - le-an - a, O - le - an - a, Far a - cross the deep blue sea,

REFRAIN: O - le, O - le - an - a,_____ O - le, O - le - an - a,

O - le-an - a, O - le - an - a, That is where I'd like to be.
O - le, O - le, O - le, O - le, O - le, O - le - an - a.

2. Oleana, that's the place,
    That is where I'll settle down;
    It's a place where land is free
    And money trees grow all around.

3. Corn and wheat grow to the sky,
    All according to the plan;
    Sheep and cows do all the work
    And fish jump in the frying pan.

4. There the crops just plant themselves,
    There the sun shines night and day;
    Harvest time comes once a month,
    But farmers only sing and play.

5. Ole Bull will play for us,
    Play upon his violin;
    And we'll sing and dance together,
    Happier than we've ever been.

Add a countermelody.

O - le, O - le, O - le-an - a O - le - an - a!

Bellflower Song

FOLK SONG FROM CHINA

"BELLFLOWER SONG" (BELLFLOWER TARYONG) FROM FOLK SONGS OF CHINA, JAPAN, KOREA. EDITED BY BETTY W. DIETZ AND THOMAS CHOONBAI PARK. COPYRIGHT © 1964 THE JOHN DAY COMPANY, INC.

Some people came from far away to live and play and work in our land. They brought their own songs with them. This song was sung by young girls.

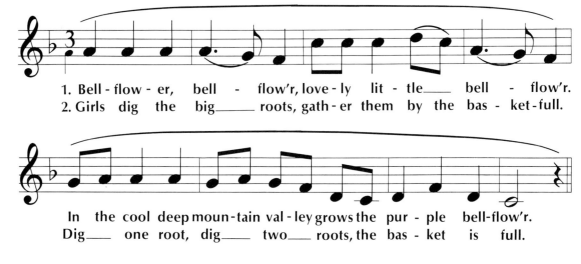

1. Bell - flow - er, bell - flow'r, love - ly lit - tle___ bell - flow'r.
2. Girls dig the big___ roots, gath - er them by the bas - ket-full.

In the cool deep moun - tain val - ley grows the pur - ple bell-flow'r.
Dig___ one root, dig___ two___ roots, the bas - ket is full.

REFRAIN

E he___ ya, E he___ ya, E he ya.

3. *E he ra nan da,* Life is so wonderful!
   You make my warm heart melt, Oh, my sweetheart.

Play one of these parts as others sing "Bellflower Song."

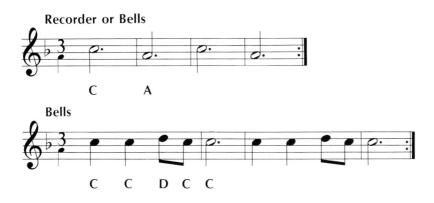

Recorder or Bells

C   A

Bells

C   C   D C   C

223

Fish Counting Song

In this fish-counting song, the fishermen mark each set of ten fish with a stick. Then they count the sticks to find out how many fish were caught that day.

There goes— one, There go— two, There go—
three, There go— four, There go— five,
There go— six, There go— seven, There go—
eight, There go— nine, There goes a stick.

Try this part on recorder or bells. Notice the measures with sound and the ones with silences.

Recorder or Bells

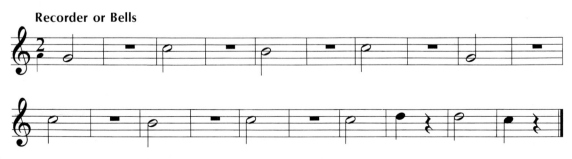

224

Cindy

SOUTHERN BANJO TUNE

After a hard day's work, people like to play. This song used to be a favorite when people gathered for a party.

Make up your own tambourine part to play as others sing.

1. I wish I was an ap - ple, A - hang -in' on a tree;
2. She took me to her par - lor, She cooled me with her fan,

And ev - 'ry time my Cin - dy passed She'd take a bite of me.
She swore I was the pur -tiest thing in the shape of mor - tal man.

You ought to see my Cin - dy, She lives a - way down South;
I wish I had a nee - dle, As fine as I could sew,

She is so sweet the hon - ey bees All swarm a - round her mouth.
I'd sew that gal to my coat - tail, And down the road I'd go.

REFRAIN

Get a-long home, Cin - dy, Cin - dy, Get a-long home, Cin - dy, Cin - dy,

Get a-long home, Cin - dy, Cin - dy, I'll mar - ry you some day.

225

A Yankee Ship

NEW ENGLAND SEA SHANTEY

In the days of the old sailing ships, the sailors gathered around the hatches to sing and dance and to tell tall tales.

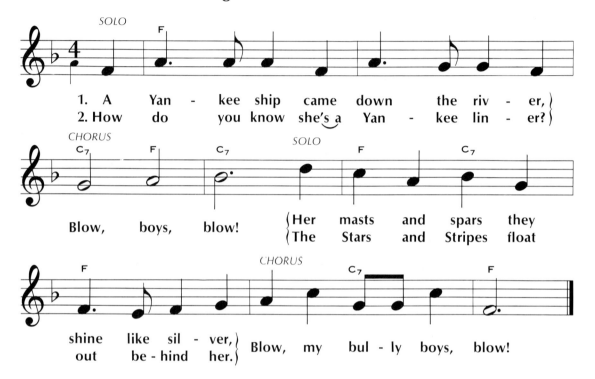

SOLO

1. A Yan - kee ship came down the riv - er,
2. How do you know she's a Yan - kee lin - er?

CHORUS

Blow, boys, blow!

SOLO

{ Her masts and spars they
{ The Stars and Stripes float

CHORUS

shine like sil - ver,
out be - hind her.
Blow, my bul - ly boys, blow!

3. And who d'you think is the captain of her?
   Why, Bully Hayes is the captain of her.

4. And what d'you think they've got for dinner?
   Pickled eels' feet and bullock's liver.

5. Blow, boys, blow, the sun's drawing water;
   Three cheers for the cook and one for his daughter.

6. Then blow, my bullies, all together,
   Blow, my boys, for better weather.

Recorder

226

Goin' Down the River

RIVER SHANTEY

FROM STEAMBOATIN' DAYS BY MARY WHEELER, COPYRIGHT 1944, LOUISIANA STATE UNIVERSITY PRESS

Loading riverboats was hard work.

Men sang as they loaded bags of corn and bales of cotton onto the boats.

Singing helped the men work together to get the job done.

1. I'm goin' down the riv - er be - fore long, oh, Ba - by,
2. I'm goin' where the chil - ly winds don't blow, oh, Ba - by,

Goin' down the riv - er be - fore long.
Goin' where the chil - ly winds don't blow.

I'm goin' down the riv - er be - fore long.
I'm goin' where the chil - ly winds don't blow.

3. I'm goin' where the sun will shine on me . . .

4. I'm goin' where ev'rybody knows my name . . .

5. I just heard that river steamboat blow . . .

227

Sailing in the Boat

AMERICAN SINGING GAME

In New England, the kitchen in a large farmhouse was often used for dancing on Saturday night.

1. Sail - ing in the boat when the waves roll high,
Sail - ing in the boat when the waves roll high,
Sail - ing in the boat when the waves roll high,
Wait - ing for a sail - or girl to come by'm by.

REFRAIN
Choose a part - ner, sail a - way, Choose a part - ner, sail a - way,
Choose a part - ner, sail a - way; We don't care if we sail all day.

2. Sailing in the boat when the waves roll high, (*3 times*)
   Waiting for a sailor boy to come by'm by. *Refrain*

3. Four in the boat, and the boat goes round, (*3 times*)
   Swing that sailor girl that you've just found. *Refrain*

4. Eight in the boat, and it won't go round, (*3 times*)
   Swing that sailor boy that you've just found. *Refrain*

228

New River Train

AMERICAN FOLK SONG

1. I'm rid - in' on that New Riv - er train,_____
2. ■ Dar - ling, you can't love_____ one,_____

I'm rid - in' on that New Riv - er train;_____
■ Dar - ling you can't love_____ one;_____

_____ Same old train that brought me_____ here
You can't love one and have an - y fun,

Goin' to car - ry me back a - gain._____
Oh,_____ dar - ling, you can't love_____ one._____

3. You can't love two and still be true . . .

4. You can't love three and still love me . . .

5. You can't love four and love me anymore . . .

6. You can't love five and take them for a drive . . .

7. You can't love six and play any tricks . . .

8. You can't love seven and pine for eleven . . .

9. You can't love eight, it's a most unhappy fate . . .

10. You can't love nine and still be mine . . .

11. You can't love ten, so begin the song again.

229

The Tiny Boat (El Barquito)

ENGLISH WORDS BY ROSEMARY JACQUES

FROM CANCIONCITAS PARA CHIQUITINES BY EMMA H. JIMENEZ AND CINCHITA M. PUNCEL. © 1969 BOWMAR/NOBLE PUBLISHERS, INC., LOS ANGELES, CALIFORNIA.

FOLK SONG FROM MEXICO

People came to this land bringing songs that helped children learn to count. This song will help you learn to count in Spanish.

1. Oh, there was once _____ a boat, _____ a boat that was so ti - ny,
2. It drift - ed one, two, three, four, five, six, sev - en weeks up - on the o - cean,

Oh, there was once _____ a boat, _____ a boat that was so ti - ny,
It drift - ed one, two, three, four, five, six, sev - en weeks up - on the o - cean,

Oh, there was once _____ a boat, _____ a boat that was so ti - ny,
It drift - ed one, two, three, four, five, six, sev - en weeks up - on the o - cean,

No mat - ter how hard it huffed and how hard it puffed, it could-n't stay on course!

1. *Había una vez un bar,*

    un barco chiquitito. (3 times)

   Que no podía, que no podía,

    que no podía navegar. (2 times)

2. *Pasaron uno, dos, tres, cuatro, cinco,*

    seis, siete semanas. (3 times)

   Que no podía, que no podía,

    que no podía navegar. (2 times)

A Gust of Fall Wind

CHINESE-AMERICAN FOLK SONG

Some people who came to this land brought songs about nature—about the wind, the frost, the dew.

A gust of_____ fall wind, blow - ing cold;

A fall of_____ white dew turned to frost.

The cruel frost freez - es each blade_____ of grass,

And the grass - hop - per dies in his grass - y nest.

Choose one of these parts to play on bells.

231

The Hole in the Bucket

AMERICAN FOLK SONG
11

Here is a muscial conversation between Liza and Georgie.

In the early days, songs like this one helped boys and

girls make light of their chores.

G: There's a hole in the buck - et, dear Li - za, dear Li - za;
L: Mend the hole, then, dear Geor - gie, dear Geor - gie, dear Geor - gie;

There's a hole in the buck - et, dear Li - za, a hole.
Mend the hole, then, dear Geor - gie, dear Geor - gie, the hole!

G: With what shall I mend it,

L: With a straw, then,

G: If the straw be too long, then,

L: Cut the straw, then,

G: With what shall I cut it,

L: With a knife, then,

G: If the knife be too dull, then,

L: Whet the knife, then,

G: With what shall I whet it,

L: With a stone, then,

G: If the stone be too rough, then,

L: Smooth the stone, then,

G: With what shall I smooth it,

L: With water,

G: In what shall I fetch it,

L: In a bucket,

(*Spoken*) *G: There's a hole in the bucket!*

Add an Autoharp part that uses only one chord, G.

Strum on every strong beat.

232

There Are Many Flags

TRADITIONAL   WORDS BY MARY H. HOWLISTON

11

Have a parade! The beat of the music will help
everybody march together.

There are man - y flags in man - y lands, There are flags of ev' - ry hue;

But there is no flag, how - ev - er grand, Like our own Red, White, and___ Blue.

REFRAIN

Then hur-rah for the flag, our coun-try's flag, Its stripes and its white stars, too,

For there is no flag in an - y land Like our own Red, White, and___ Blue.

Add a drum part.

Play throughout.

Recorder Fingering Chart

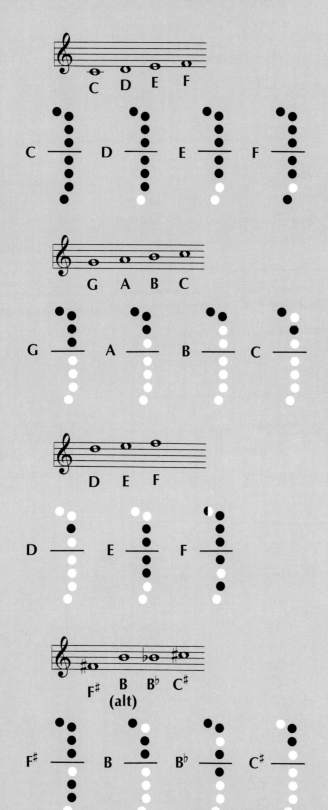

Glossary

accent   A single tone or chord louder than those around it

accompaniment   Music that supports the sound of a solo performer

atonal   Music in which no single tone is a "home base" or "resting place"

beat   A repeating pulse that can be felt in some music

cadence   A group of chords or notes at the end of a phrase or piece that gives a feeling of pausing or finishing

chord   Three or more different tones played or sung together

composer   A person who makes up pieces of music by putting sounds together in his or her own way

contrast   Two or more things that are different. In music, slow is a *contrast* to fast; section A is a *contrast* to section B.

countermelody   A melody that is played or sung at the same time as the main melody

density   The thickness or thinness of sound

dynamics   The loudness and softness of sound

form   The overall plan of a piece of music

harmony   Two or more tones sounding at the same time

melody   A line of single tones that move upward, downward, or repeat

meter   The way the beats of music are grouped, often in sets of two or in sets of three

notes   Symbols for sound in music

octave   The distance of eight steps from one tone to another has the same letter name. On the staff these steps are shown by the lines and spaces. When notes are an octave apart, there are eight lines and spaces from one note to the other.

phrase   A musical "sentence." Each *phrase* expresses one thought. Music is made up of *phrases* that follow one another in a way that sounds right.

pitch   The highness or lowness of a tone

register   The pitch location of a group of tones (see pitch). If the group of tones are all high sounds, they are in a high *register*. If the group of tones are all low sounds, they are in a low *register*.

repetition   Music that is the same, or almost the same, as music that was heard earlier.

rests   Symbols for silences in music

rhythm pattern   A pattern of long and short sounds

tempo   The speed of the beat in a piece of music (*see* beat)

texture   The way melody and harmony go together: a melody alone, two or more melodies together, or a melody with chords

theme   An important melody that occurs several times in a piece of music

tonal   Music that focuses on one tone that is more important than the others—a "home base" or "resting" tone

tone color   The special sound that makes one instrument or voice sound different from another

variation   Music that is repeated but changed in some important way

vibration   Back-and-forth motion that makes sound

Index

Acknowledgments

Credit and appreciation are due publishers and copyright owners for use of the following.

"April Fool's Day" by Marnie Pomeroy from POEMS FOR SEASONS AND CELEBRATIONS, edited by William Cole. © 1961 World Publishing Company, Cleveland, Ohio.

"Blum" reprinted by permission of G. P. Putnam's Sons from *Here, There and Everywhere* by Dorothy Aldis. Copyright © 1928, 1956 by Dorothy Aldis.

"But You Are Mine" ("Lullaby") used by permission of Institute of African Studies, University of Ghana, Legon, Ghana.

"Lewis Has a Trumpet" from IN THE MIDDLE OF THE TREES by Karla Kuskin. Copyright © 1958 by Karla Kuskin. By permission of Harper & Row, Publishers, Inc.

"Paper I" from THE COMPLETE POEMS OF CARL SANDBURG, copyright 1950 by Carl Sandburg; renewed 1978 by Margaret Sandburg, Helga Sandburg Crile and Janet Sandburg. Reprinted (or recorded) by permission of Harcourt Brace Jovanovich, Inc.

"Rain Sizes" from THE REASON FOR THE PELICAN by John Ciardi. Poem Copyright 1959 by The Curtis Publishing Company. By permission of J. B. Lippincott, Publishers.

Picture Credits

Cover: Silver Burdett
Instruments: courtesy of Dorn & Kirschner Band Instrument Co., Union, N.J. 2: *t.* Silver Burdett; *b.* Victoria Beller-Smith for Silver Burdett. 3: Victoria Beller-Smith for Silver Burdett. 5: Silver Burdett. 7: Silver Burdett. 12: Dan De Wilde for Silver Burdett. 13, 14: Silver Burdett. 18: John Bacchus for Silver Burdett. 22: Silver Burdett. 26: *t.* Cornell Capa from Magnum; *b.* Victoria Beller-Smith for Silver Burdett. 27: Victoria Beller-Smith for Silver Burdett. 28, 29: Silver Burdett. 34, 35: Victoria Beller-Smith for Silver Burdett. 38: D. Kateley from DeWys, Inc. 39: *t.* Susan Johns from Rapho Guillumette; *m.* William Carter; *b. l.* Joel Gordon from Photo Trends; *b. r.* Victoria Beller-Smith for Silver Burdett. 40, 41: Al Freni. 48: Tim Eagan from Woodfin Camp. 53: Silver Burdett. 58: Victoria Beller-Smith for Silver Burdett. 70: *t.* Norman Owen Tomalin from Bruce Coleman; *b.* Neville Fox-Davis from Bruce Coleman. 72: Victoria Beller-Smith for Silver Burdett. 80: *t. r., b. l.* Courtesy, Sheldon Jackson College, Sitka, Alaska; *m. r., t. l., b. r.* Museum of the American Indian. 80, 81: John Running. 82: *l.* John Running; *r.* Belzeaux from Rapho Guillumette. 84, 86: Silver Burdett. 86: *b. l.* Victoria Beller-Smith for Silver Burdett. 89: Silver Burdett. 96: John Bacchus for Silver Burdett. 97, 100: Victoria Beller-Smith for Silver Burdett. 108: Doug Bates. 111: Victoria Beller-Smith for Silver Burdett. 127, 137: John Bacchus for Silver Burdett. 139: *t. l.* Baldwin Piano and Organ Company; *t. r.* Hal McKusick from D. P. I.; *m. l., m.* Photo Media Ltd.; *m. r., b.* John Bacchus for Silver Burdett. 142: Silver Burdett. 148, 149: Victoria Beller-Smith for Silver Burdett. 158, 159: Silver Burdett. 162–163, 172, 173: Victoria Beller-Smith for Silver Burdett. 178: W. Bryant from Camera 5. 178, 179: Victoria Beller-Smith for Silver Burdett. 179: *t.* Silver Burdett; *b.* Jim Eversole. 184, 185: Victoria Beller-Smith for Silver Burdett. 192, 196: DeWys, Inc. 209: *t.* John Running; *b.* Tim Eagan. 218: *t.* Matt Greene; *b.* Victoria Beller-Smith for Silver Burdett.

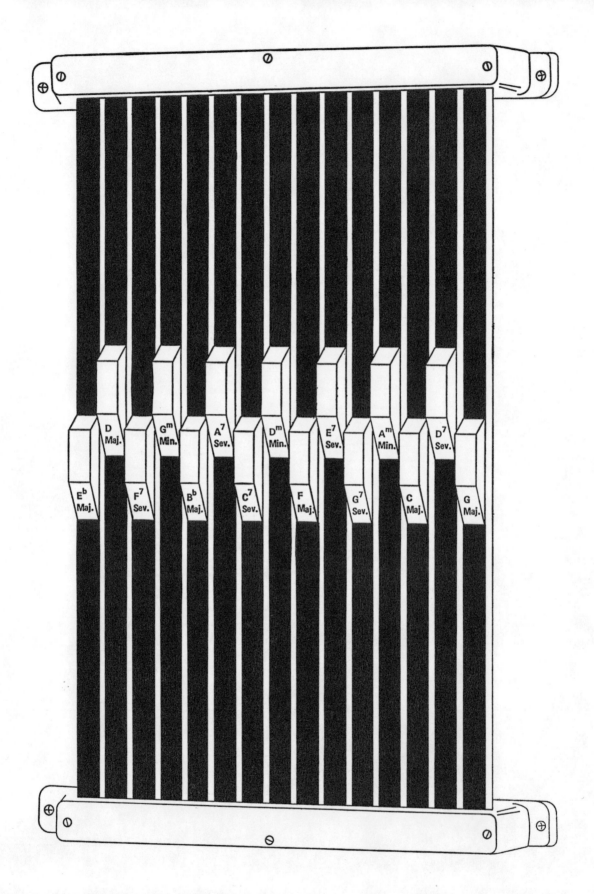